EXCEL 2026

The Most Exhaustive Guide to Master Excel Formulas &

Functions. From Zero to Expert in Less than 7 Days with Step-by-Step

Illustrated Instructions, Practical Examples, and Tips & Tricks

Scott Burnett

GET YOUR BONUSES NOW!

To walk you through the journey of learning Excel, in collaboration with Mike Collins and Linda Carter, I have created two guides on time management and productivity strategies that will help you get the most out of this book.

We believe that these strategies are vital not only in the process of learning new things, as in this case, but in all aspects of life. Indeed, they will help you achieve set goals with less effort and without wasting time.

All these bonuses are **100% free**, with no strings attached.
You don't need to enter any details except your name and email address.

To download your bonuses scan the QR code below

Table of Contents

Introduction

If you are into spreadsheets, then Microsoft Excel is the application for you. This software can help you organize data in a neat and easy to read manner and calculate different formulas and statistics. With this application, the possibilities are endless! Microsoft Office 365 has been working hard to make its products cloud-based and accessible by various methods. We all know that Microsoft Excel is very popular among top companies; therefore, having a good knowledge of the software could help you and your organization make the best use of the tool. There are many ways to simplify data with Excel tools.

Microsoft Excel is a spreadsheet tool that can be used to perform computations, graph data, and make charts. Microsoft Corporation first published it in 1985 as part of the Microsoft Office suite. It is part of the company's productivity suite of products. The software has evolved to meet the demands of a changing world, with new versions being released.

The future of Microsoft Excel will be an AI-powered software that can decide what to do based on the input it receives from the user. It will also be able to learn from a user's decisions and make more accurate predictions.

The software is available for both Mac OS and Windows, and it allows users to carry out operations such as creating pivot tables, performing basic mathematical operations, writing data with the action pen or using a touch screen monitor, unhiding multiple worksheets, and manipulating rows and columns.

Microsoft releases new versions of Excel, as a result, some of your questions might not be answered in this guide. With this guide, you'll be able to get started with Microsoft Excel quickly and discover new ways to collaborate on spreadsheets.

While there are many free Microsoft Excel tutorials online, the lessons in this book will help you understand the basic tools and functions of Microsoft Excel. You would learn how to use the Quick Access Toolbar, Ribbons, Power Query, Power Pivot, and other features to your advantage. There are many benefits of taking this book.

Microsoft Excel is a powerful data analysis and graphing tool. It can be used to create complex financial models, manage and analyze data, and generate graphs and charts. In this introductory course, you will learn how to use Microsoft Excel to create and format worksheets, enter and edit data, perform calculations, create charts and graphs, and protect Worksheets.

Features of Microsoft Excel

Microsoft Excel is a spreadsheet program widely used to analyze, organize, store, and calculate data. This application can also be used to track finances, create graphs, or store information.

Microsoft Excel is a desktop application that allows users to create and store spreadsheets, calculate numbers, and perform many other tasks. It can be used on Windows, macOS, iOS, Android, the web, and the Microsoft Surface Hub.

If you're new to Excel, you should know the basic features of this software. You can enter formulas in cells, but they must start with the equals sign. The result of an equation is displayed in the cell, and Excel automatically updates the result whenever you change a component. You can use basic formulas in Excel to replace a calculator. Each cell works with data in other cells, so you can also use them to perform calculations.

The address bar displays the active cell's address, while the formula bar lets you enter formulas in cells. The title bar shows the name of the workbook and application, and a click on an Active Cell will highlight it. The File menu has several options, including save, open, and new. You can open, save, and close new worksheets with the File menu. The "New" button offers a searchable library of templates.

The cells are the basic components of the spreadsheet, and they contain text, numbers, and dates. Cells can also be customized with different sizes, colors, and borders. Each cell has an address, which is a number or letter that represents the column or row where the cell is found. You can also move data around by dragging the border of a cell, making it easier for you to change the layout of a spreadsheet.

The spreadsheet has changed the way we work in so many ways. It has made it possible for us to do calculations that were not possible before. We can now keep track of our finances or inventory more efficiently than ever before.

Filtering data is another essential feature of Excel. Filtering enables you to hide data that is not relevant. You can use filters to quickly find data by color or value. You can also filter rows based on specific features. Once you know these features, you'll be well-prepared for any data analysis project. If you're unfamiliar with Excel, these features are an absolute must!

1.1 Cell

If you're unsure about what a cell in Excel is, here's a quick overview. A cell is a rectangular area within a spreadsheet. Each cell can be identified by a name or an address, which is derived by combining the Column Letter and the Row Number. A cell can contain Labels, Numbers, Formulas, or Functions. If you're not sure how to refer to a cell, alternative cell names can provide a shortcut for the jump to a specific section of the spreadsheet.

Each cell in Excel has a name based on the column and row it is found. For example, if you click on cell "C " in column C, you'll see the name "C5", which means the cell is located in column C and Row 5. The cell address appears in the Name box. If you're unsure of what a cell name means, you can search for it by highlighting the row and column headers.

The CELL function can return the value of a specific cell, as well as its label prefix. When a cell contains text, it returns a single quotation mark (') or double quotation mark (""), or a caret or backslash ('). When a cell contains nothing, it returns "empty text. " The cell name also refers to the active sheet, which may differ from the sheet where the formula is located.

1.2 A work or spreadsheet

A work or spreadsheet in Microsoft Excel is a document that is created using the Excel software. It is a document that contains formulas, charts, and other data. A workbook can be collaborative, meaning you can add comments to cells or ranges of cells or open and close comments as needed. You can also add formatting to your work or spreadsheet by using the Insert tab. This tab provides all the options you need to format your work.

A work or spreadsheet in MS Excel is made up of rows and columns, and can contain different data types. For instance, one row may contain information about a stock price, while another might contain information about the stock market. Each cell in an Excel spreadsheet can be a different type of data, and the user can sort them into a specific column or row. When using the Excel spreadsheet software, it is important to remember that each row and column has its own cell address, so you need to know each cell address when using formulas.

When you use Excel, you will often encounter words like "worksheet" and "column". A workbook is a document that has many different columns and rows, and each row and column has an associated cell reference. This API lets you insert or manipulate cells in your workbook, and change the width and height of those rows and columns as necessary. Using a worksheet in Microsoft Excel has many benefits for business owners and individuals.

1.3 Worksheet

In Excel, a worksheet is a collection of cells that are organized together in a workbook. A worksheet's name is usually the same as the document's name; however, a workbook could contain multiple worksheets. These different worksheets can be accessed by selecting a sheet tab at the bottom of the document, where a plus sign is located. Click the sheet tab to give the worksheet a specific name and move or rename it.

Besides text, an Excel workbook can also contain pictures, charts, diagrams, buttons, and more. All of these objects are stored in the sheet's draw layer, so if you're using this software to build a presentation, you can insert charts, pictures, or diagrams into the worksheet. Moreover, you can add images to your workbook by dragging them to the appropriate place.

A worksheet is a collection of cells, which can contain data, text, or formulas. The cells on a worksheet are usually rectangular-shaped and arranged in a grid pattern. In MS Excel, each cell in the workbook is identified by its column and row numbers. Worksheets are named based on the contents of each cell, and the names can be changed. You can also add and delete individual worksheets in a workbook by using the context menu.

1.4 Workbook

Basically, a workbook is a file in the Microsoft Excel software, and this file type can be saved in many ways. For example, you can save it to a new location, make a backup copy, or save it in a different format. You can also view and edit a workbook using the File menu.

A workbook is a collection of sheets, and a sheet is made up of rectangular cells. Individual cells are identified by their cell references which are vertical column letters and horizontal row numbers. Worksheets are stored in the same workbook, and you can add or delete them as needed. Workbooks can contain thousands of worksheets.

Workbooks can be used to save, edit, and organize your work. If you use multiple workbooks, you can hide and display each worksheet separately. You can also hide individual worksheets by clicking on the tab holders. For example, if Sheet2 has too many worksheets, you can delete them. Alternatively, you can edit the entire worksheet by clicking on the row header.

Adding worksheets to a workbook is as easy. Workbooks are used in a professional environment. Worksheets are specifically intended for specific data sets, while a workbook is an all-purpose data set. Workbooks contain worksheets of various sizes and shapes. A workbook can contain as many worksheets as you want.

Excel's Graphical Design

Excel's Database Functionality

Excel Tools & Functions

Home

Insert

Page Layout

Formulas

- Data
- Review
- View
- Shortcut Menu
- Basics in Spreadsheets
- Formula Bar
- Header & Footer
- "Find & Replace" Function
- Password Protection
- Data Filtering
- Sorting Data
- Formulas that Are Built-in
- Make Various Graphs (Pivot Table)
- Instantly Edit the Result
- Auditing Formulas

1.5 Excel's Graphical Design

A great way to create a beautiful spreadsheet is to learn to customize the design of your work in Excel. The Excel software has many features similar to those of PowerPoint. You can insert images and shapes, use gradients, and even customize your charts. People will often judge a book by its cover, so take the time to design the spreadsheet the way you want it to look. There are many benefits to spending some time on the visuals of your project.

Excel has a variety of interactive features for representing data in graphs. For example, there are Charts, Shapes, Clip Arts, Pictures, & Smart Arts.

1.6 Excel's Database Functionality

MS Excels Database Functionality allows you to perform complex data analysis tasks. Unlike other database programs, Excel does not let blank cells in its database. This is because it divides the data into rows and columns; therefore, having an empty cell will prevent Excel from performing basic data analytics functions on disconnected data. Even a simple filtering operation will fail if the data is disconnected. Each row and column of data in a database is a record. Some of the features include tables, pivot tables, sorting, grouping, filtering, slicers, and data validation.

1.7 Excel Tools and Functions

Getting started with Excel is easy. After you download the software, you can start using it immediately. However, it would help if you familiarized yourself with some standard tools and functions to get you started. These include the formula bar and address bar. Both of these areas are used to enter formulas into cells. The title bar shows the name of the workbook and application. The file menu offers shortcuts such as save, open, and new. Excel tools and functions help in performing efficient calculations and boosting the Application Features. Some examples include Formulas, VBA Macros, Hyperlinks, Add-ins, Spell Check, Security, and Conditional Formatting.

1.8 Home

Microsoft Excel has a tab for "Home" that contains a number of different commands. The home tab can be used to make changes to the spreadsheet. The home section of MS Excel consists of font size, font color, font types, color for background, color palette, spacing, formatting choices and styles, cell addition and deletion, and editing options.

1.9 Insert

The Insert tab is made up of features like table shape and type. This tab can be used to add photos and numbers, header and footer choices, tables, maps, sparklines, equations, formulas, and symbols.

1.10 Page Layout

In MS Excel, you can define the layout of a page by clicking on the Page Layout tab. Here, you can adjust the margins for the header and footer. This tab is helpful when your data is long and will span several pages. The default page layout in Excel includes both a header and footer, and you can change their placement if you'd like. You can also add or remove a column title in the page layout to make it easier to read.

You can modify the size of the page layout and change it to your desired size. If you want to add a page break, select the blue line next to the cell where you wish the page breaks to appear. By default, this option is hidden, so be sure you check it if you need it. Alternatively, you can enable Black and White and select Low Print Quality to speed up the printing process.

Changing the page size is one of the easiest ways to change the format of a document. In Microsoft Excel, you can change the margins on the document. First, choose the size and orientation of the page in the page layout. You can also change the document's orientation by clicking on the orientation option. Once you have selected the format, click OK to confirm the settings. Next, choose the font you want to use for the document. The page layout option includes themes, alignment, and page configuration choices.

1.11 Formulas

A formula is a mathematical expression that tells the computer to perform a specific operation on a cell's value. Formulas are used in a spreadsheet application to calculate large data in a relatively short amount of time. A formula will calculate simple arithmetic like the sum of a range of cells, rows, or columns. You can use an example in Excel by typing the formula SUM(A1:A3). If you're using Excel for Mac, you'll use the same formula, but it's important to remember that formulas always begin with an equal sign. Since MS Excel can generate tables with a vast volume of details, one can use this function to apply formulas to the table and get faster results.

1.12 Data

There are three types of data in MS Excel and they are; numerical, text, and logical data. These data types are used to organize information, label cells, and separate data into categories. They also make for great headings and names. Logical data type is one of the most powerful tools in Excel, and it displays values as TRUE or FALSE. Usually, logical data is returned as a result of a calculation.

The MS Excel Data Tab allows you to work with spreadsheets that contain formulas and data. There are also options for filtering, sorting, and manipulating the data. Additionally, you can import external data into your spreadsheets. The Get External Data button will help you import data from many different sources. The Power Query feature also lets you combine data from multiple sources. If you are looking for more advanced formatting options, you can also use the Advanced tab.

1.13 MS Excel Review Tab

The MS Excel Review tab can be used to comment on a document. You can check spelling and grammar, translate a sentence, and do research. This tab also has several other features, such as inserting comments, tracking changes, and proofreading. The review tab is also helpful for document protection. It helps you check your work before you send it to someone else. If you have a complicated document, you can use this tool to add and remove comments.

1.14 View

In MS Excel, the View tab allows you to compare two open files. It positions two windows horizontally by default. However, you can change this composition by clicking the Arrange All button. This button opens a dialog box that gives you options such as Vertical, Horizontal, or Cascade. Horizontal and vertical placements place sheets next to each other. Cascade overlaps windows from top to bottom. In this way, you can view a large number of worksheets simultaneously.

1.15 Shortcut Menu

In the Excel Ribbon, you can find several commands that will open a shortcut menu. These include the Paste Special command, which you can use when copying text or cell content.

1.16 Basics in Spreadsheets

Learning how to use MS Excel is an important skill for anyone. Spreadsheets are a versatile tool for creating different types of documents. For example, you can use them to track your business's sales and financial records. There are several sample questions for MS Excel that will help you improve your computer awareness score. Whether you want to get started with Excel or you're a seasoned pro, there are many resources available in this book to help you learn the basics.

1.17 Formula Bar

The MS Excel Formula Bar allows you to edit the formula content of a cell. You can use this tool to change the contents of a cell without having to make the entire modification yourself. The formula bar can also be used to modify the value of a cell's contents.

While it is possible to hide the formula bar, it is not recommended. To remove or reveal the formula bar if it has been obscured by error, select Excel Options at the right (bottom) of the menu that displays by pressing the Office button. Select the 'Advanced' option and tick the box for the Display formula bar underneath Display to view the formula bar. When you're done, simply press Ok.

1.18 Header & Footer

You can add a header and footer to your document using MS Excel's features. This feature is accessible by clicking the Header & Footer button on the Insert menu bar. The header or footer will be placed above the text you've entered in the header box. You can center, left-align, or right-align the text you added in the header or footer. The footer can contain program-generated information and can be customized as needed.

1.19 "Find & Replace" Function

If you need to replace some text or data in an Excel spreadsheet, you can do so by using the Find & Replace Function. You can access this feature in the Home tab of the spreadsheet and open the Find and Replace dialog box. Select the Replace option in the drop-down menu. Type the text you want to replace into the field, then click Find Next to move to the next instance. Alternatively, click Find All to view a list of locations.

1.20 Password Protection

To prevent unauthorized access to an Excel workbook, you can use MS Excel Password Protection. While trying to access a password-protected file, you will be prompted to enter a password. Use a password that you can remember and avoid using a general password that is easy to guess; you can thwart most password guessing attempts by using capital letters. Once you've set a password for the workbook, you can edit, print, and save the file.

1.21 Data Filtering

In MS Excel, data filtering can be helpful for various purposes. This type of filtering is often used to create a table of data, such as a customer list or a product sales list. Data filtering can also be used to make your list easy to manage. Once you understand how MS Excel data filtering works, you'll be able to use it more effectively.

For sorting ranges in Excel, there are two commands:

- AutoFilter: This provides a selection-based filter with basic parameters.

- Advanced Filter: It uses more complicated parameters.

1.22 Sorting Data

If you have a list of data, you may find it useful to sort them by color or by some other criterion in ascending or descending order. Microsoft Excel provides a number of ways to do this. You can copy a column/field, change its color or font style, or assign an icon to each cell. These options are available in the Data tab on the left side of the toolbar. In the middle of the toolbar, you'll find the Sort option.

1.23 Formulas That Are Built-in

If you are looking for ways to enter formulas into your spreadsheet, you might want to know about built-in functions and Formulas. Functions are used to enter standard or complex formulas. They start with an equal sign ("=") and use cell references as their format. For example, the Sum function adds values in a range. To use this function, type =sum(H2:H25) and press enter. Gridlines are horizontal lines that separate cells. If you are printing your spreadsheet, make sure to turn on the appropriate layout options. Other built-in formulas may include averages and minimums.

1.24 Make Various Graphs (Pivot Table)

How do you make different graphs or pivot tables in MS Excel? Depending on your needs, you can add different types of graphs and tables in Excel. You can change the appearance of each graph by changing its label. To edit the label, click on it and select Edit. You can also change the font, size, and colors of each graph or table. You can add additional rows and columns to the Pivot Table if you're creating a chart.

1.25 Instantly Edit the Result

How do I edit a result in MS Excel? In many cases, it is easy to make mistakes and forget to enter data. That's where this function comes in handy. It allows you to add comments to a cell or a range of cells. You can also open and close comments. Then, click OK to save your changes. You can even edit the result in the cell itself.

If you want to edit the result of a formula, the Excel program offers a feature that allows you to Instantly Edit the Result. Double-clicking a formula cell will bring you into the edit mode, where you can change the value of the formula. You can also change the formula cell reference. Once you have changed the cell reference, you can edit the formula in the cell. It will automatically change the cell references after copying it.

1.26 Auditing Formulas

If you use MS Excel regularly, you're probably aware of its extensive list of MS Word and Excel Auditing Formulas. These powerful tools allow you to check for errors and improve your data in Excel. You can also use a tool that draws special red arrows all over your worksheet. These tools are available for free, but you may need to purchase a subscription to keep up with the latest features.

Getting Started with MS Excel

You are about to start using MS Excel; as a newbie, you might not know how to begin. Here are a few tips to help you get started. First, you have to open a blank workbook. A workbook is a file that contains one or more worksheets. Excel automatically gives each workbook a file name depending on how many you open. For instance, if you open a new workbook, you might get a file name like "Book1". In addition, the screen you see may vary depending on the version of Excel you are using.

Secondly, you should learn how to manage the various menu items in Excel. Most of the standard menu items are accessible by clicking on tabs. It would help if you also learned how to manipulate page layout, as this will determine the overall look of your work. You can adjust how the Ribbon looks and feels by adjusting the Display Options. Some versions will install additional tabs to help you get started. Generally, the Ribbon is a responsive interface. Therefore, if you find that it takes up too much screen space, you can minimize the Ribbon to make it more user-friendly.

One of the best ways to save time is to use keyboard shortcuts. Most computer users are used to using a mouse or touchpad. However, many of us do not think of the world without these tools. The keyboard shortcuts for copying, deleting, and moving are all familiar. They save us time and can even save us money! For example, pressing the ESC key while selecting a cell will remove the animated border. Another keyboard shortcut that you may want to learn is typing in the cell with the arrow keys. When you do this, Excel will insert a row above the row you clicked. Likewise, pressing F4 will insert additional rows or columns.

This course is an excellent introduction to spreadsheets and will help you prepare for the Microsoft Office MO-200 exam. You will learn to manage numerical data, create multiple sheets, analyze data, and work with tables, charts, and graphical objects. It will also give you the skills to enhance your workbooks and perform independent tasks. When you learn the basics of the program, you'll soon be able to use it to your advantage.

Once you know the basics of Excel, you can experiment with formatting and data analysis. You can edit cell content with the AutoFill and AutoCorrect features. Both save you time when typing and help you avoid typos. AutoCorrect is available by clicking on the Tools tab and selecting the AutoCorrect option. You can also activate AutoFill to save time when typing numbered lists. Simply click on the Fill and Series command and press F2.

Using the VLOOKUP function is an excellent way to move data between two sheets. This option will allow you to copy data from another file to Excel. This method works best with similar files, such as CSV files. For newer versions, you can simply select all cells and copy the data from another file. Once you've completed this process, you'll notice that you're taken to the graphical user interface. You have to select the option to return to the worksheet.

1.27 Open a New Workbook

There are many ways to open a workbook in MS Excel. You can open a workbook from the Start menu by clicking File and selecting Open. Alternatively, you can click the Office button and choose Open. Regardless of which method you use, you'll need to follow the same basic steps. Once you've done so, you'll be able to easily access the second file from a new instance of Excel.

The first step to creating a new workbook in Excel is to choose a template. By default, Excel opens a new workbook with three blank worksheets. You can choose a workbook template if you're starting from scratch. Another way to open a new workbook is to select File > New from the menu bar, or press Ctrl+N or Command+N and double-click on the "blank workbook" option. Make sure to know what you're doing and how to align your columns and rows.

Alternatively, you can choose a workbook already in use. In this case, the new workbook will be named Book1, and you can close the existing one. Then, you can open the new one by selecting it from the To Book list box. You can even choose to store the current workbook online using Microsoft's Skydrive service. Just make sure to save the workbook in a safe place.

1.28 Building a Worksheet

This section will show you how to build a worksheet in Microsoft Excel. A worksheet is a collection of cells that contain text, data, and formulas. It is a great way to keep track of your personal finances and business records so you can present them to whomever needs to see them. There are several steps involved in building a worksheet. In this section, we'll focus on the first one, creating a new worksheet. However, you may find this section helpful for other purposes as well.

If you open the work area of Excel, you'll notice that it has rows and columns. Each column can be used for a specific month, while rows for expense types. Click the tabs to separate data. Once you're done, you'll see the different tabs and columns. If you're working with a large spreadsheet, you can also use the Symbols tab to insert non-standard characters into cells.

Once you've created the worksheet, you'll want to add data verification. This helps prevent accidental subtractions or additions that can ruin your spreadsheet. Moreover, data verification is an excellent way to build a strong spreadsheet foundation. Once you've created your spreadsheet, you can begin filling in data. It's important to remember that you can only build a small part of your spreadsheet at a time.

Once you've completed the spreadsheet, open it in Microsoft Excel. This will open the sheet in Excel. Once you've done this, click the "X" button to save it to your workbook. You can also change the formatting of your spreadsheet by double-clicking the cell and modifying the values. You can then move on to the next step.

1.29 Formatting a Worksheet

There are many ways of formatting a worksheet in MS Excel. You can choose the default look of the column headings or customize their background color. To change the default look, select the items by clicking on them or hold down the Ctrl key and click on them again. Next, click on the Format headings tab and change the formatting of the selected item. Save the changes. Formatting a worksheet in MS Excel is easy!

You can change the font size and type to enhance readability. In the Home tab, click the Font tool. If the font you are currently using is Calibri, size 11, you can change it to something else. To change the default font, ensure that you have no cells selected. To change the font, click on the Font button. You can also change the color and style of the font. Choose a different font for each column or row.

If you are using a series of columns, you can use alignment to make each row and column title stand out. It also makes text aligned within cells easier to read. Additionally, you can use borders to categorize the data and highlight the most important details. By choosing the proper alignment for the columns and rows, you would create a more organized and effective sheet. You can even add a border around the worksheet to draw its structure.

1.30 Editing and Proofreading a Worksheet

In MS Excel, editing and proofreading your Worksheet will allow you make changes to the document. You can use spell check to ensure that all words are spelled correctly. Then, you can move or replace any of the text that you have entered. Also, you can check the spelling of a word by clicking the Spelling button in the Format menu. Finally, proofreading your Worksheet will ensure that it is free of errors.

To proofread a worksheet, you can use a red pen or highlight any changes you've made. This will allow you to track your changes, including the cells and margins. Then, you can choose whether to accept or reject those changes. This book also explains how to track changes, add comments, and compare two versions of a worksheet before preparing a final version for sharing.

You can also check spelling by clicking the Spelling option in the Review Tab. Click on the Spelling option to check the spelling of the word. Excel will start correcting any spelling errors from the current cell point all the way to the end of the worksheet. You can also choose to turn off the AutoCorrect feature which automatically corrects mistakes when you type. It also offers you suggestions for synonyms and antonyms of the word.

If you're not sure how to proofread your worksheet, consider using the Spell Check option to spot errors. It works as a spell check for your spreadsheet but doesn't flag all of your changes. By using this feature, you'll be able to quickly identify errors and make corrections to your spreadsheet in a few minutes. When you're proofreading your worksheet, remember to take breaks to relax.

1.31 Managing Worksheet in MS Excel

There are many ways to manage your workbooks in MS Excel. In this section, you will learn how to arrange workbooks on screen. You can also learn about the Names property of the Worksheet class. Names allow you to add, remove, or modify names within a worksheet. For more information, read the Names section. You can also arrange worksheets with their title bars visible. Once you have the desired arrangement, click the Arrange All command in the View tab.

In general, you should organize your worksheets in a top-to-bottom sequence. Exceptions to this rule include input and results worksheets. If possible, put these worksheets at the top of your spreadsheet, since this will increase clarity for users. Avoid circular references and criss-cross dependencies, which detract from comprehensibility. Instead, use top-to-bottom naming conventions, which will help you keep your spreadsheets organized and easy-to-understand.

In addition to naming your worksheets, you can also create links between them. This is useful when you need to share information between different sheets, such as a financial statement. When you are ready to share your workbooks with others, ensure you save them first. You can save your workbooks by clicking the Save button on the Home ribbon or by choosing the Save option from the File menu. You can also print and share your workbooks.

Managing Worksheet in MS Excel allows you to organize multiple workbooks at once. Managing worksheets is not difficult once you know how to use the right-click menu. It can be difficult to see the entire worksheet when using multiple worksheets, but Excel's worksheet manager makes it easier. It also allows you to easily change the order of your worksheets, add new ones, and delete old ones. You can also use the Backstage view to view workbooks in other locations.

1.32 How to Print a Spreadsheet in Microsoft Excel

There are many ways to print a spreadsheet in Microsoft Excel. Whether you are printing out a report or a spreadsheet for your own use, you can always switch to your default printer if necessary. To switch between printers, simply click the File tab in the Ribbon and choose "Print to a new printer. "

One way to print data on one page is to change the worksheet's page orientation to landscape. By doing this, you can adjust the margins and page size to make the data look good on a single page. This option is useful if your data is too small to be read but can affect the layout. To hide rows or columns before printing the spreadsheet, right-click and select "Hide rows or columns. "

Alternatively, you can also print a selection of cells or ranges of data in a worksheet. If you don't provide a range to print, Excel will print the entire worksheet. If you do not provide a range, select the name of the range from the Name Box pull-down menu. To print the selected area, click on the Office Button located in the top left corner of the Excel window. Select the desired areas to be printed.

To print a range of cells in a worksheet, click the "Print Selection" button on the File tab. Then, select the cells you want to print. In the column headings, you can choose rows and columns to print. For the table, click the first and last sheet tabs. Then click the "Print" button. By clicking "Print", you will see a preview of the selected cells.

1.33 How to Use the Ribbon in Microsoft Excel

If you want to know how to use the Ribbon in Microsoft Excel, you're in the right place. Here you will learn how to customize the Ribbon Panel in your spreadsheet. First, right-click the Ribbon Panel to bring up an options dialog box. Click the Customize Ribbon menu option. You can click the Developer tab and deselect any tabs you don't want to show. Then click OK to apply the changes.

The Ribbon is available in several ways. You can simply click on a tab to hide it, but you can also choose to hide it permanently. If you don't want to hide the Ribbon permanently, you can click the arrow in the lower-right corner of the tab bar. You can also choose to automatically hide the Ribbon, which hides it when you aren't using it. Alternatively, you can click Control+F1 to show the Ribbon.

The Ribbon is customizable, and you can add commands to individual tabs or groups. You can also change the order of tabs and groups. In addition, you can rename tabs and show or hide hidden ones. You can also make your tabs context-sensitive, so they only show up when you select an item. Regardless of how you use the Ribbon, you'll be glad you took the time to customize it.

Once you've customized the ribbon, you can customize your workspace. Click the Auto-hide ribbon option to prevent the ribbon from appearing, or click Show Tabs and Commands to reveal the ribbon. Click the Customize Ribbon button to add or remove commands and groups that you don't need. By doing this, you'll have a more convenient experience with Excel. You'll also be able to customize the ribbon in ways that will make your work easier.

1.34 Creating Custom Ribbon Tabs in Microsoft Excel

You've come to the right section if you've always wanted to add custom groups to your Excel ribbon. Custom groups allow you to add commands to the ribbon that don't already appear on the default tabs. These groups are called "subgroups, " and they're useful for adding more functions to your spreadsheet. If you don't want to use any of the default tabs, you can create custom ones for yourself.

To customize the Ribbon, go to the Options window and then click the Customize Ribbon option. In the Customize Ribbon section, select the tabs and groups you want to hide. Uncheck the boxes that you don't want to display. Then click OK. When you're finished, click the Save button. Then, you'll see a customizable Ribbon, complete with tabs for common tasks. After customizing the ribbon, you'll be able to use it to make your spreadsheet the way you want it.

The Ribbon contains individual buttons. Click them to use an option. Most commands require selected content or a location in the worksheet to be active. Most buttons are color-coded, and group names refer to the group. The Font group, for example, is highlighted in blue. Alignment is highlighted in red. Some buttons contain further options, including borders, text orientation, and merge and center. These options are also available in the Custom Tabs and Groups section.

The Ribbon can be hidden or visible depending on your preferences. If you want to hide the ribbon altogether, simply right-click the tab bar and uncheck the option to collapse the ribbon. Then, you can customize the ribbon by double-clicking the tab bar and choosing "Extras. " If you want to display the ribbon on a specific worksheet, you can also click the button to make it expand. Another option is to press CTRL+F1 and select the custom tabs you want to display.

1.35 How to Hide and Re-Show the Microsoft Excel Ribbon Bar

First, understand what the Ribbon Bar is. This bar consists of individual buttons that you can click on to use different options in your spreadsheet. Most of these commands require that you have selected certain content and be in a specific position on the worksheet to perform them. Many of the buttons are organized into groups that include other options such as borders and text orientation. Some buttons also have further options, such as merge or center. Read on to discover more about this bar and how it works.

Depending on your needs, you can customize the Ribbon. To do this, go to the Options dialog box and click Customize the Ribbon. In this dialog box, you can remove or add custom tabs and reorder the tabs. You can also hide or show specific tabs. You can also customize the tabs that show up when you select an item in the Ribbon. You can even remove the Page Layout tab and make it default.

After you understand the basics of the Ribbon, you can customize its appearance. Right-click on the Ribbon Panel and click the Customize Ribbon menu option. In the options dialog box, deselect the Developer tab. You can now select Customize the Ribbon and customize its appearance. On the Developer tab, you can access advanced features, such as VBA macros, ActiveX controls, and XML commands. By choosing this option, you can customize the appearance of the Ribbon by renaming the tabs in the Developer tab.

You can hide and re-show the Microsoft Excel Ribbon Bar in various ways. First, you can choose to display only Tabs and Commands. You can also opt to hide the Excel ribbon area and see only the Tabs and Buttons. To re-show the Ribbon, press Control+F1.

Next, you can move commands from one place to another. The built-in tabs are located on the far left and right sides of the ribbon, and you can choose to place custom tabs anywhere you like. In addition, you can hide tabs you don't use by un-checking their check boxes and clicking OK. In this way, you can organize the Ribbon Bar in the way you prefer. It can also be arranged by group.

A basic understanding of the Ribbon is essential for working with the software.

1.36 Using Worksheets to Manage Data in MS Excel

MS Excel allows you to create multiple-page spreadsheets, called workbooks, with pages containing various types of data. Worksheets exchange information with each other, and they can be organized into groups. This chapter explains how to manage worksheets within a workbook. For example, you can use the Find and Replace command to replace the text in one worksheet with data from another. However, you may be interested in a more advanced approach.

There are different ways you can make copies of your worksheets, one of which is by opening the Worksheet tab and dragging it to a new location. You can then change the location of the new worksheet and hide it. You can also drag it to the right side and rename it. You can also copy and paste your workbook to another location. However, you need to do this carefully because it can result in confusing information and formatting. Instead, learn how to manage the worksheets in MS Excel so you can make the most of your data.

To highlight a range of cells, click on the highlighted cells. You can also open other worksheets in the workbook. Many of these functions are accessible from the Excel Ribbon. The ribbon is the upper area of the screen, containing tabs corresponding to different commands in the spreadsheet. Once you have created a workbook, you need to navigate to it. You can find this menu in the top-left corner of your screen.

1.37 Doing Calculations in MS Excel

Doing Calculations in MS Excel is simple if you understand the basics. Using logical operators is the most common way to perform mathematical operations in Excel. Operators are symbols that define the relationship between values and cell references. Examples of logical operators are the plus and minus signs, the forward slash, and the asterisk. Excel follows a specific order for these operations. If you have a table with two columns, you can use the precedence table to do more than one calculation for each row or column.

You can also use a built-in function in Excel. This feature allows you to perform calculations using large data sets. In this case, the formula will be executed in cell D8. The formula will recalculate each time the number in cell D8 changes. If you've used formulas in MS Excel before, you'll know that Excel reads them in the natural order of arithmetic operation, starting from left to right.

In addition to using formulas to perform calculations, you can use functions in Excel to perform more complex calculations. A formula consists of a series of commands that instruct Excel to perform a particular calculation. A function, on the other hand, is a pre-written formula that Excel automatically applies. The average function, for example, calculates the sum of a group of numbers by counting their digits and dividing by their value. Functions can be embedded in formulas, or you can use the default values to perform calculations.

1.38 Carrying Out Measurements

If you are looking for a way to carry out measurements in MS Excel, then read this section! In this section, you will learn how to use the rulers provided in Excel to accurately measure items in your worksheet. Excel provides rulers for column width and row height, as well as graduations for both the horizontal and vertical sheet rulers. To change the default units of the rulers, simply change the Display section and select "Inches. "

The first step in carrying out measurements in MS Excel is to add the data to the data model. This is similar to inserting a PivotTable. Select the data range you would like to work with, then select Insert PivotTable. Make sure to mark "Add this data to the data model" when asked. After selecting this field, you should see a dialog box that will show you the column width and measurement type.

To calculate the mean, median, and standard deviation, you must use the formulas in MS Excel. Then, you need to convert the text values to numbers by using the LEFT function and multiplying them with 12.

1.39 Customizing the Ribbons Tabs

If you want to customize your Excel program, you can easily do so by customizing the Ribbons Tabs. In the Options dialog box, you can select Customize Ribbon. To change the appearance of the Ribbon panel, click on the Developer tab. After that, click Options. You should now see a new window. Click Customize and then choose the commands you want to be displayed on the Ribbon Panel. You may want to change the order of the commands on the Ribbon Panel.

You can also rename the built-in tabs and groups. Unlike the custom tabs and groups, you cannot rename Excel commands. Once you've customized the tabs, you can rename them. The name of the item that you want to rename appears on the Customize the Ribbon window. If you're going to rename the tabs, you need to make sure to create new custom groups.

To customize the ribbons tabs in MS Excel, click on the command icon that looks like a small triangle. This will bring up a dialogue box where you can name the new tabs. Once you choose a name, you can then customize the custom tabs by selecting a symbol. Once you're done, click Add, and your new tabs will appear. It won't look like you're trying to create a new group.

You can also choose the command that you'd like to display on the ribbon. Typically, you can add or remove tabs by double-clicking them. You can also collapse the ribbons and re-enable them by selecting the 'Collapse Ribbon' option. This way, you can maximize the space of your worksheet while still maintaining the customization of the ribbon. The same method can be used to collapse and expand the ribbon.

1.40 Choosing a Color Scheme

MS Excel offers several options for customizing the look of your workbook. One option is to use a color scheme. Color schemes are sets of eight coordinating colors for text and objects. You can apply a color scheme to a single sheet or workbook. Changes to the color scheme will also affect the objects and text behind a list. The theme is a way to set colors for specific elements in the workbook.

There are numerous ways to choose the perfect color scheme. The first step is to understand the purpose of the scheme. Do you want to use one color or many? What are the main colors you want? You can use a color wheel to determine how colors relate to each other. Colors that look good together are complementary or analogous. Using the color wheel can help you pick a color scheme that suits your needs.

Once you've mastered the basics of color theory, you can create your own custom color palettes. Most versions of Excel have a default color scheme that uses the Office theme. However, if you're looking to customize the look of your workbook to make it stand out, you can also create a custom color scheme and store it for future use. However, you won't be able to set a custom theme as the default color in MS Excel, so you'll need to create a default workbook template first.

1.41 Formulas Settings

You can change the default formulas in MS Excel by using the Formulas Settings menu. To change the default formulas, select the appropriate option for your use. For example, if you are working with a table, you can choose to automatically recalculate it for all cells except those in the Data Tables. The data table is not an ordinary Excel table. It is a tool for performing scenario analysis. It is found on the Data tab. To access the What-If Scenarios tool, click on the button in the Data tab. The Calculation setting is also available on the Excel Options menu. This menu can be found under File.

When changing your formulas, you can choose to recalculate the entire workbook or select a specific sheet. By default, Excel uses the Maximum Change value to determine when an iterative calculation has converged. However, you can change this value to 0.0001 or 0.001, which will prevent it from continuing the calculation. If you don't want to recalculate the entire workbook, you can recalculate it manually.

If you use the Table Names setting, you can choose to automatically reference specific rows or columns in a table. This feature minimizes typing errors by providing a drop-down list of names, functions, and text strings. You can also select a display trigger or text string. It's a simple way to get started with Excel. For more information, check out our tutorial on Excel. You can find the right formulas for your spreadsheet.

1.42 Save Your Preferences

Once you've finished customizing the way your spreadsheets look, you can save them as Excel templates to use next time you create a new spreadsheet. This way, you'll avoid having to manually adjust these settings each time you create a new spreadsheet. And, if you haven't yet done so, you can even save your settings for each worksheet in advance. Here's how:

To do so, open the Options dialog box and choose the option to Save As. A list of recently used locations will be displayed on the left. You can then choose the name of your workbook and the type of file you want to save. Click the Save As button and then choose your preferred file type. Save As will open the dialog box so you can choose where you want to save the file. Choose the location where you want the file to be saved.

Excel features a tabbed ribbon system to make it easier for you to find these options. It contains multiple tabs and several groups of commands. These tabs are used to perform the most common tasks in Excel. Clicking a tab will display more commands. You can also adjust the Display Options of the Ribbon. Moreover, some programs can install additional tabs in Excel, known as add-ins. It's important to save your preferences in MS Excel so that you can use them again.

Basics of The Microsoft Excel

1.43 Inserting Rows and Columns

To insert a new row or column, you must select the cell in the row or column below the new insertion. Alternatively, you can insert more than one column by holding Shift and clicking on the header of the column you want to insert. Selecting multiple cells in a row will result in the new rows or columns being placed above and between existing rows or columns. This method will also work with the columns but is more difficult.

The process of inserting new rows and columns in MS Excel is almost the same. Once you have selected a cell, you can click the Insert button in the Cells area. Select the row or column that you want to insert and click OK. Once the new row or column is added, you can adjust the reference to the next cell. Then, simply select the cell below the row or column to insert it into.

In order to insert a row or column, you can either use the keyboard shortcut CTRL++ (plus character) or press the keyboard CTRL+SHIFT+= (equal sign). Once you have chosen the row or column, you can then right-click the cell or click the arrow keys to select it. After you have selected a column, you can now insert a row or column in Excel. You can then modify the data in the sheet and use its properties.

1.44 Using Pivot Tables for Data

Using Pivot Tables for Data is a great way to summarize and analyze large amounts of data. Rather than building a separate report for every category, a pivot table lets you group data by category, break it down by year, month, and so on. You can even create charts to illustrate your data. Using pivot tables is not limited to financial analysis. For example, you can use them to compare sales between two different products or to analyze your sales over time.

The basic concept behind a pivot table is simple. You can select a column total and then use the Pivot Table to calculate a percentage. By doing this, you can filter your data by month to find the top performers by product. The pivot table also calculates total sales by percent, allowing you to view sales by month, year, and product. Once you have created your pivot table, you can easily view your data with its new functionality.

After you create your pivot table, you can use PivotTable Options to automatically format empty cells. You can also format numbers in any number format. However, you should be aware that some number formats disappear if you edit the PivotTable, so you should be prepared for that. You can then proceed with the analysis. If you have collected data from many different sources, you can easily create a pivot table from them.

1.45 How to Use Autofill

Autofill in MS Excel can be a useful feature if you're creating a new spreadsheet and need to type in data repeatedly. Autofill will complete most cells and even months and years as column headers for you. To use autofill, just select two cells in your spreadsheet and type in the data you want. The autofill feature will then copy the formula and place it into the selected cell. You can even use Autofill to fill in whole columns with data from the adjacent cells.

There are many settings you can use in Autofill. You can choose to have it copy the values of a selected range without formatting. To do this, double click the + sign and choose "Fill." This will open the Fill box with many options. Select "Fill without formatting" to copy only the value. If you don't want the formatting to be copied, choose "Fill only values."

The AutoFill Options dialog box will appear. To use the fill handle, you must first select the cell you want to fill. Once you do, a fill handle will appear on the cell. The fill handle is located next to the AutoFill item on the mini-toolbar. To change the AutoFill option, click "AutoFill Options" on the shortcut menu. You can also use AutoFill Options to select the type of data you want AutoFill to insert.

1.46 How to Use Filters

To create a list with the correct columns, you must first open the Data tab in the worksheet. Next, click the drop-down arrow next to the column header. You can filter data by text or color or by equals, starts with, ends with, contains, and does not contain. Similarly, you can filter data by column. You can also combine multiple filters and sort data. Once you have finished sifting through the data, you can save your selection and return to the previous list.

To make your data selection more efficient, you can use the Excel filter function. The FILTER function returns only cells that meet specific criteria. It is not available in older versions of Excel. It's a feature only available to subscribers of Microsoft 365. The regular data filter filters the existing dataset, while the Excel advanced filter extracts the data to a different location. In addition to simple and complex criteria, you can also use the Advanced filter for complex filtering.

To remove a filter, you need to click on the drop-down icon. Clicking on it will select the data. Using it is a powerful feature that will allow you to select specific information. You can also copy the filtered information to use in your work. You can also delete the filter and return to the previous one. Once you have sorted your data, you can delete the filter. There are many advantages to using the filters in Excel.

1.47 How to Sort in Microsoft Excel

If you're looking for ways to organize your data in a simple, quick, and clean way, sorting in Microsoft Excel is one of the best options. There are several different ways to sort data in Excel, and we'll cover each one below. To get started, select the column you want to sort by. Click the arrow next to "A to Z" on the toolbar. You can also choose a different font color or cell icon.

To sort by column, click the corresponding cell in the data column. In Excel, click the Sort & Filter option in the Data tab. Similarly, click the Editing group on the Home tab. For easier access to the Sort dialog, you can use the shortcuts Alt-A-S-S. Before starting, make sure the My Data Has Headers option is set to "yes. "

When arranging data by column, you can use a custom list to organize the data. Then, you can sort each column according to its value. The same goes for arranging cells by format. To sort by column, use the "Column" button to select a specific cell. Once you've selected a cell, select the "Sort" icon in the right-hand column. From there, select the option you want to use.

SORT is a dynamic array function that spills data to adjacent cells. Sorting by column is the default behavior, but if you want to sort data by column and row, you can use the by_col and by_row arguments. The sort_index parameter is optional, and the default is one. You can type the value you want to sort by in the corresponding column and row. This option is helpful if you need to sort data by multiple levels or in multiple rows.

1.48 How to Remove Duplicates

If you have a complicated spreadsheet, removing duplicates might be challenging. In this section, we'll go over how to remove duplicates from your spreadsheet in a simple and effective manner. Before beginning, make a backup of your data file. Then, follow these steps to delete duplicates in

Microsoft Excel. First, select the data in the duplicate cell. After that, press the Ctrl+Z keyboard shortcut to undo your actions.

Once you have selected your data, you can copy it to another sheet or the same one. By selecting Unique records only, you can copy the values, and only one duplicate will remain. You can also select the cells that share the same fields, such as name and address. Once you have copied the values, click on the "Remove Duplicates" button on the Data tab. It is located in the top-right corner of the sheet.

Another method is by selecting a specific cell in the range and removing all the duplicates. You can also choose a column to base duplicates on if you want to. By default, all columns are checked. To filter and copy values, you can use Advanced Filter. If you have to remove duplicates from a certain range, use the Advanced Filter option. This option can help you find the exact values you're looking for.

Selecting a column header is a great way to find and remove duplicate values in a table. By doing this, you can filter for column headers and remove column headers. By doing so, you can remove duplicate values in a table quickly and easily. After all, you'll be glad you took the time to learn how to remove duplicates in Microsoft Excel. So, start making use of it today!

1.49 How to Paste Special

There are many ways to copy and paste data in Microsoft Excel. In this section, we'll cover several ways to copy and paste data. If you want to copy or paste a cell formula, for example, you can choose to copy the formula as a value. You can also copy a cell's comment or annotation. But before you paste a cell, make sure to first select the cells you're going to copy.

To paste numeric data, you need to use the Paste Special feature in Excel. This action will add or subtract values in the cell range. It will also multiply or divide the values, and will skip empty cells. This option is located in the Clipboard section of the Ribbon on the Home tab. In Microsoft Excel, you can right-click the cell to select it and choose Paste Special. Once you've selected it, you'll see a drop-down arrow next to the Paste Special button.

If you want to paste numbers with destination formatting, you'll need to use the Paste Special command. Select the destination cell's number format and select OK. If you want to keep the formatting, the result is a number on row three. If you paste numbers in row three, they will retain the formatting in row one. However, if you paste a cell from row one to row three, the pasted numbers will remain unchanged.

1.50 How to Use Text to Columns

Whether you need to separate content into two or more columns in MS Excel, you can use the Text to Columns feature. This powerful feature can be used to convert numbers and dates into text and separate them into different columns. It also allows you to convert international number formats and date formats into text. To use the tool, all you need to do is follow a few simple steps.

First, select the data you want to split. You have two options to choose from: Delimited and Fixed width. Select the delimited option. You can also select the text qualifier to wrap the string and mark it as text. This way, you'll be able to preserve text blocks. You can change the width or position of the text blocks if necessary. Alternatively, you can change the width of the columns.

The next step is to select Text to Columns in the Data tab. You can format the columns to be either wide or narrow or pick a specific destination cell. Choose the format you want. Once you've chosen your desired format, you can use Text to Columns in MS Excel to display the new columns in a table. It's as easy as that! Once you have set up a new column, you can now use it to display data from other sources.

One of the most common uses for Text to Columns is to extract the first few characters of a name. For example, if you want to export data from an Excel document with multiple lines of information, you can use a custom filter. First of all, you can enter the name of the person you want to extract. If you're looking for a first name in a column, you can simply enter the first name of that person and click on the filter icon in the destination cell.

1.51 Format Painter

You can paste the formatting of a cell into another worksheet with the Format Painter tool. The Format Painter tool is available in the Clipboard group on the Home tab. To use it, click the Format Painter icon and then double-click on a cell. Then, choose the range of cells you wish to copy the formatting from. You can then paste the formatting on another worksheet or workbook. However, note that you can only paste the formatting of one worksheet to multiple worksheets or workbooks.

This tool is located near the Paste option on the Clipboard on the Home tab. The Format Painter icon changes to a paint brush when you click it. Simply select a cell to paste the formatting, and the Format Painter will copy the formatting to the next cell or row. This is a very effective way to make quick changes. You can use it to change the font size and color of a cell. It also lets you change the cell border and align text.

Another useful tool for formatting your Excel sheets is the Format Painter. This tool lets you copy and paste formatting from one cell to another, and then paste the same formatting onto the next. This tool is especially useful for making a datasheet look better. It allows you to highlight headers, set column widths, wrap text, and eliminate gridlines. It makes it easier to read and makes the data in a worksheet more attractive.

MS Excel Formulas

For most marketers, trying to organize and analyze spreadsheets in MS Excel will seem like hitting a brick wall. As you physically recreate columns and scrawl long-form math on a sheet of paper, you think to yourself, "There has to be a simpler way to do this."

In this way, Microsoft Excel may be picky. On the one hand, it's an excellent tool for analyzing and tracking marketing outcomes. If you don't have the experience, it's easy to come across as working against you. But when you know how to use the tools and functions of Microsoft Excel, it will run hundreds of important formulae for you, saving you from having to trawl through thousands of cells on your desk.

1.52 The Difference Between Functions and Formulas in MS Excel

When dealing with MS Excel, it might be difficult for you to know the difference between formulas and functions. Both are used to complete calculations, and their use is highly beneficial. Formulas are often more general and are better suited for quick tasks, while functions are more specific. In this section, we'll explain the difference between formulas and functions, and how they're used in MS Excel. Let's begin by defining what a function is. A function is a pre-defined calculation. While a formula requires a developer to write, functions are based on the same set of rules.

Formulas are essentially user-defined mathematical equations, whereas functions use predefined calculations. A formula can be simple or complex, but a function will execute more sophisticated computations. Functions in Excel allow you to perform a variety of calculations. These are pre-defined formulas that perform various mathematical, statistical, and logical operations. All you need to do is enter an equal sign (=) in the cell where you wish to perform a calculation, and a function will do the rest. Once you've entered the correct syntax, click the 'function' button on the formula bar. This will open a list of functions, as well as the syntax required for each one.

A function can be used to solve engineering problems, create financial models, or use a single mathematical function. In this way, it's similar to using a calculator to perform calculations. If you're working with a formula to solve a problem, you'll want to make sure you know what you're doing.

You can look up an example of a formula on the Internet. A formula is an expression that instructs Excel on how to calculate a certain value in a cell, but a function is a pre-defined function that you can call at any time. The SUM function, for example, computes the sum of two cells depending on their values. Although a formula can have several arguments, it must start with an equal sign.

1.53 What is Excel Formula?

The first question that comes to your mind when you think of MS Excel is: What is an Excel formula? There are many different types, but this section will address the most common ones. In addition to the question of what an Excel formula is, you will learn how to insert a formula in a cell. The formula text will appear in the cell and in the formula bar. You can have as many as 1,024 characters in the formula text, and it will always refer to it's cell.

You may use Microsoft Excel formulae to detect associations between values in your spreadsheet's cells, do mathematical calculations on those values, and then return the result to the cell of your choice. Formulas such as sum, subtraction, ratio, aggregate, average, and event dates/times may be executed automatically.

Microsoft Excel formulas allow you to calculate numbers while making sense of large amounts of data. By learning a few key formulae in Microsoft Excel, you may boost your productivity and reduce the risk of measurement errors. To help you start, here's a collection of Microsoft Excel formulae.

There are a few complicated formulae, but a good one shouldn't be. In addition, some of the most useful formulae can help you fully utilize the features of Microsoft Excel.

One of the most basic formulas in Excel is the SUM formula. This formula finds the sum of two values and can be entered in either a cell number or actual numbers. The SUM function will return a result, even if the calculation has errors. Some examples of SUM formulas include addition, subtraction, multiplication, and division. They can also be used to calculate dates and percentages.

A formula is defined as an expression that works with a variety of values in a given range of cells or even one cell. A formula is a mathematical expression that tells the computer to perform a specific operation on a cell's value. Formulas are primarily used in spreadsheet applications, where they enable calculations of a large data set in a relatively short amount of time. A formula will calculate the sum of a range of cells, rows, or columns. You can use an example in Excel by typing the formula SUM(A1: A3). If you're using Excel for Mac, you'll use the same formula, but it's important to remember that formulas always begin with an equal sign. For example, to calculate the sum of cells from B1 through B4, we use the formula =B1+B2+B3+B4 or say =SUM(B1:B4).

1.54 In Microsoft Excel, How to Insert Formulas:

To create an equation, you must first insert a formula in a cell. In Excel, the first character of a formula is an equals sign. It can contain any type of constant, calculation operator, or asterisk. It can also contain a value or a cell reference, or even commands to add, subtract, or perform other actions. You can use as many as 8192 characters for a formula.

In Excel, you can link formulas to multiple worksheets. This means you can refer to cells in other workbooks in your formula. To do this, you simply select the formula cell and drag the bottom-right corner to another cell. Excel will copy the formula and adjust the cell references. This step is similar to pasting text. However, when pasting a formula into a cell, it will not paste the formula.

You can also find formulas using Excel's formula icon library. This handy catalog contains formulas related to common subjects. Each formula icon is highlighted with a long red rectangle. You can browse the list and select the one you want to use. If you're not familiar with the formula icons, you can look for one related to your subject matter. If you're unsure, you can always look for a formula by using the Search Bar.

Once you have selected a cell, you can then enter a formula into it. Once the formula has been entered, the value will appear in the cell. You can edit the formula in the cell if you wish. To do this, simply double-click the cell to display the formula and make the necessary changes. If you're not confident with entering a formula, you can always go back and type it again.

You may be unsure what the "Formulas" tab on the top navigation toolbar of Microsoft Excel signifies. In the current versions of Microsoft Excel, the horizontal menu — seen below — assists you in finding and inserting Microsoft Excel formulae into specific cells in your spreadsheet.

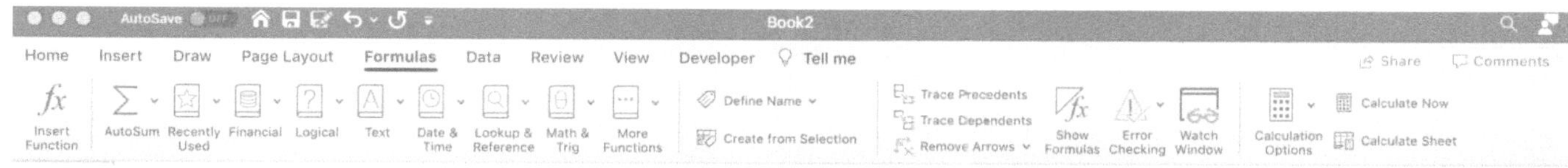

The more you utilize Microsoft Excel formulae, the quicker you'll be able to remember and execute them by hand. Nonetheless, you may use the symbols above as a reference guide for formulae that you can search and return to as your spreadsheet abilities grow.

In Microsoft Excel, formulas are sometimes known as "functions." To add one to your spreadsheet, pick a cell where a formula is needed and tap the "Insert Function" button on the far left to search for basic formulae and functions. The browser window would look like this:

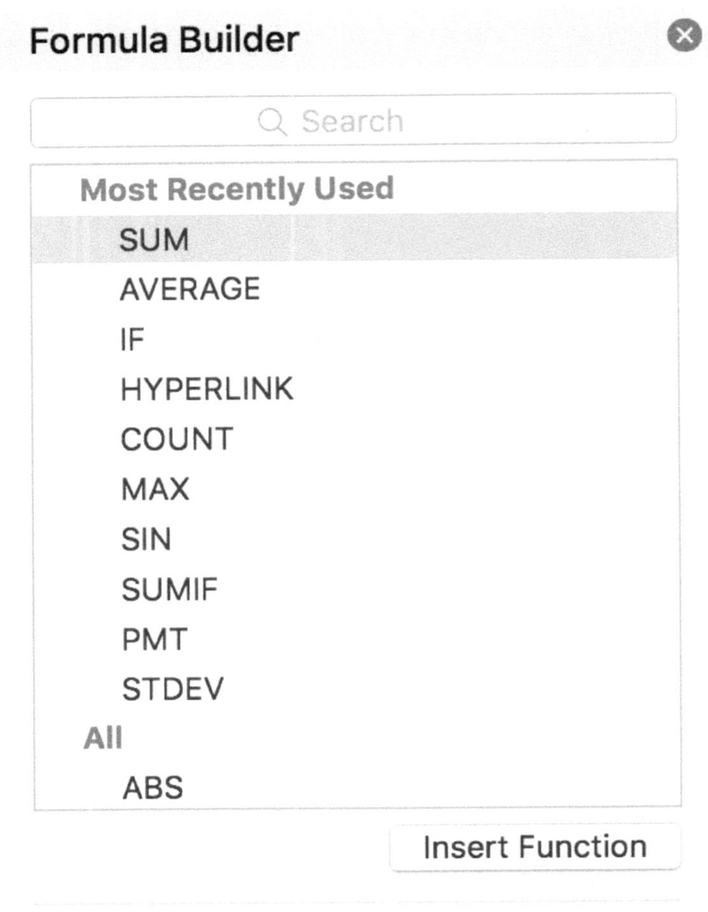

As seen in the window above, click "Insert Function" until you find a formula that works for you.

To insert the formula by Simple Method

To input, a formula, follow the steps below.

1. Select a cell to work with first.

2. To notify Excel you wish to enter a formula, use the equal sign (=).

A3		fx =A1+A2	
	A	B	C	D
1	2			
2	3			
3	5			

3. As an example, type the formula A1+A2.

4. Change the value of cell A1 to 3.

5. Excel updates the result of the calculation in column A3 automatically.

A1		fx 3	
	A	B	C
1	3		
2	3		
3	6		

To Change a Formula

When you click a cell in Excel, the value or formula of that cell appears in the formula bar.

1. Click on the formula bar and make the required modifications to update a formula.

2. Press the Enter key on your keyboard.

SUM		✕ ✓	fx	=A1-A2
	A	B	C	D
1	2			
2	3			
3	=A1-A2			
4				

A4		✕ ✓	fx	
	A	B	C	D
1	2			
2	3			
3	-1			
4				

Priority of Operator

The default sequence in which Excel calculations are performed has been configured. If a part of the formula is included in parenthesis, it will be calculated first. After that, it calculates multiplication and division. Excel will add and subtract the remainder of your computation for you when you're finished. Consider the illustration on the right.

A4		fx	=A1*A2+A3

	A	B	C	D
1	2			
2	3			
3	1			
4	7			
5				

To begin, Excel multiplies the values (A1 * A2). Excel then adds the value of column A3 to this result.

A4		fx	=A1*(A2+A3)

	A	B	C	D
1	2			
2	3			
3	1			
4	8			
5				

How to Create a Formula by Copying and Pasting in MS Excel

If you need to create a formula in MS Excel, you can copy and paste a cell with a formula. When you copy a cell, the reference to the original cell will be preserved. By copying and pasting a cell that has a formula, you can easily create a new formula with the same formula in a different cell. Moreover, you can also paste a cell with a formula to another column or row.

Select the cell containing the desired range to copy a single cell, then right-click and choose Copy. You can also press CTRL + C or click on the Paste Options button if you're using a keyboard. Alternatively, you can use the Paste icon in a different column. After copying a cell, click on the paste icon and paste the range into Column F. If there are reference data gaps, you need to repeat the copying process.

Another method to copy a cell value is to press Control+D or Control+Shift+'. When copying a cell, you can choose to copy the contents of the cell or just paste the formatting. Using Control+C and Control+V will allow you to copy a cell and paste it into another cell. You can also copy a cell with a range of cells.

The cell references for each cell where you duplicate the formula change automatically when you copy it.

Perform the tasks given below to have a better understanding of this.

1. In cell A4, enter the following formula.

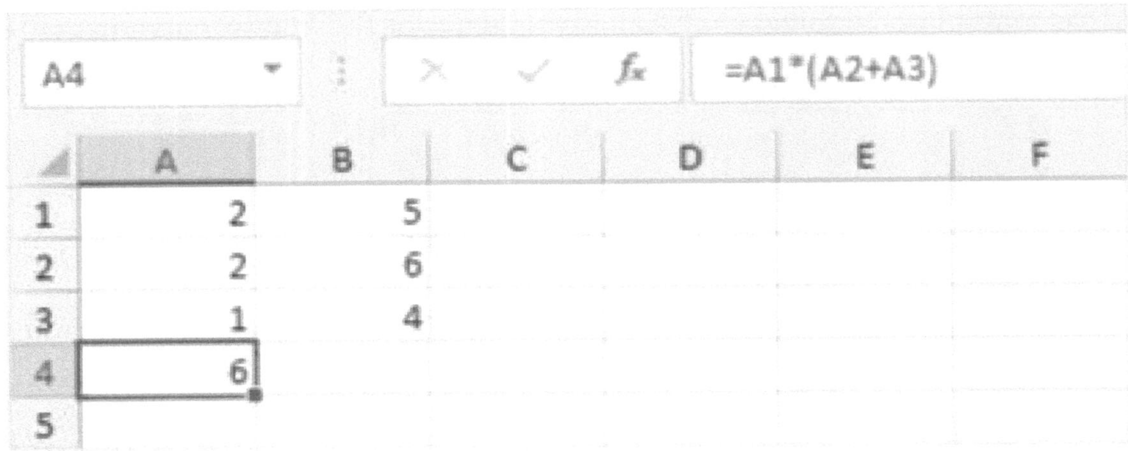

2a. Right-click cell A4, then choose Copy and Paste from the 'Paste Options menu.

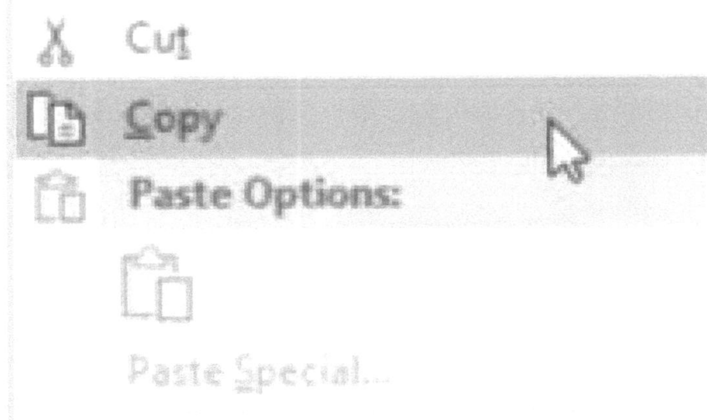

2b. You may drag the formula to cell B4 and drop it there. Cell A4 is chosen, and its bottom right corner is clicked and dragged to cell B4. It's a lot less work and yields the same result!

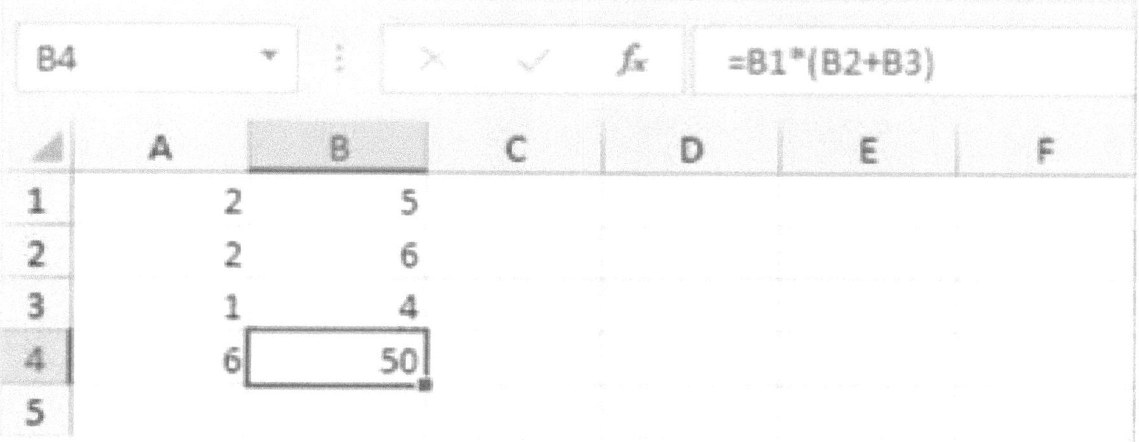

Result. In cell B4, the formula refers to the numbers in column B.

Incorporate the Formula Inserting a Function Key

You may utilize additional Excel functions by using the Insert Function command on the Formula bar (the one with the FX). When you click the Insert Function button in Excel, the Insert Function dialogue box appears. Then you may use its options to find and choose the function you want to use and specify the parameter or arguments the function needs to do its computations. Each function has the same structure. For instance, consider SUM (A1:A4). The name of this function is SUM. The portion within the brackets (arguments) indicates that we're providing Excel the A1:A4 range. This function is used to sum cells A1, A2, A3, and A4.

To add a function, follow the steps below:

1. Pick a cell.

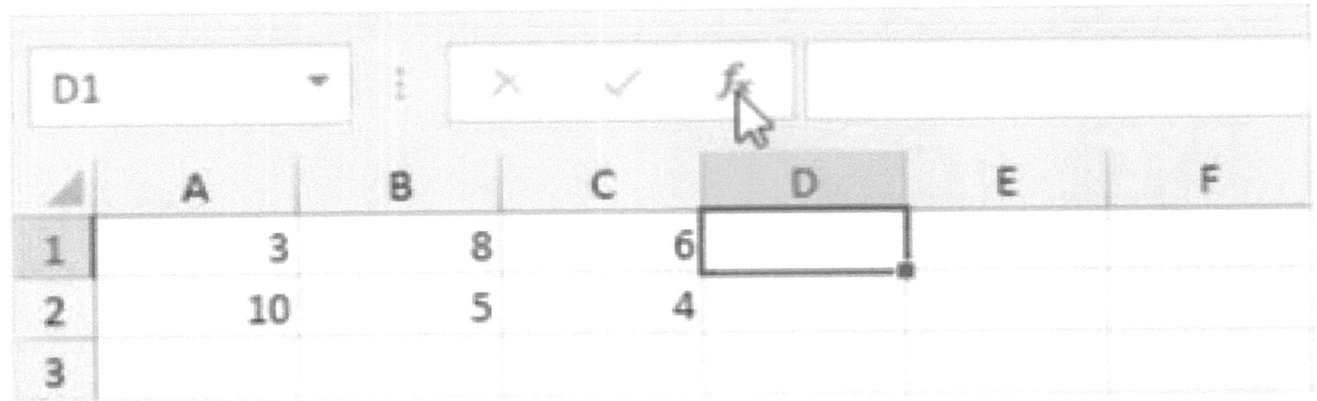

2. From the drop-down option, choose Insert Function. The 'Insert Function dialogue box appears.

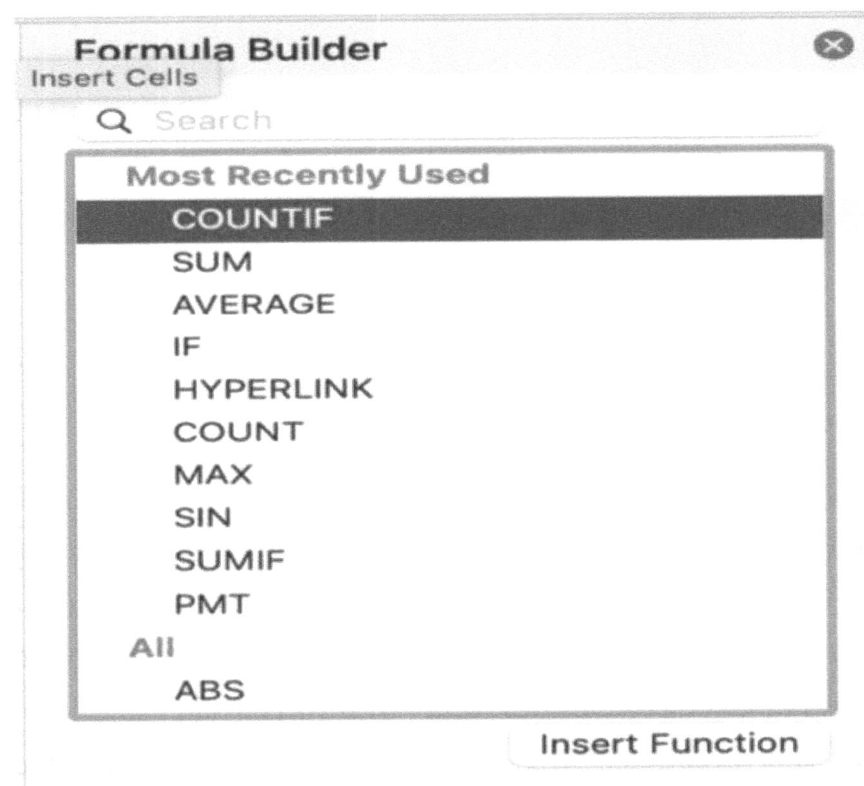

3. Look for a function or choose one from a list of options. For example, choose COUNTIF from the Statistical category.

4. Click INSERT FUNCTION.

5. The 'Function Arguments' dialogue box displays.

6. Click on the A1:C2 range in the Range box to choose it.

7. In the Criteria box, type >5 and click OK.

8. COUNTIF counts the number of larger-than-five cells in a row.

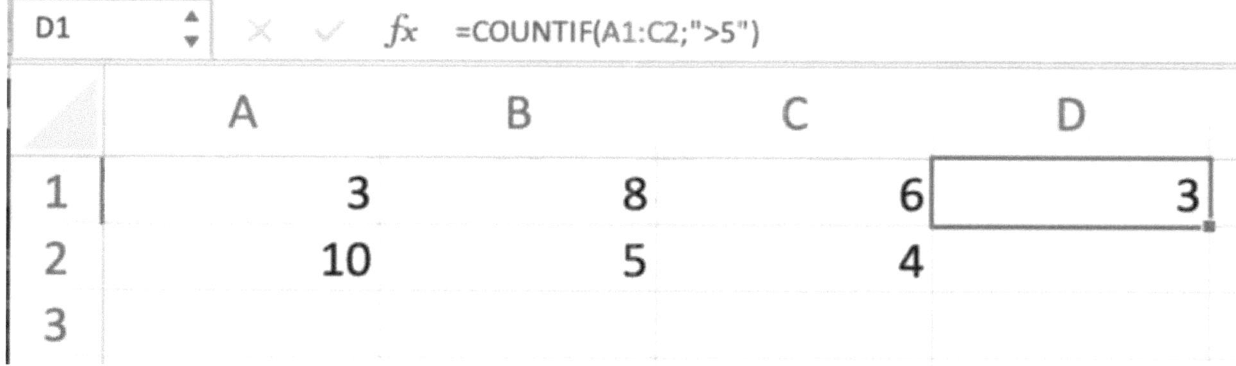

AutoSum Option

An AutoSum function is a useful tool for fast and routine tasks. You can choose the AutoSum option in the far-right corner of the Home page. Then, using the mouse pointer, expose more previously hidden formulae. In the Formulas tab, you'll see this option as well.

1.55 How to Use the Most Common or Basic Formulas in Microsoft Excel

We've compiled a list of useful formulae, shortcut keys, and other handy tools and features to help you get the most out of MS Excel (and save a lot of time).

The formulae in this section are for Microsoft Excel 2022. Some of the functions listed below may be at a different location if you're using an earlier version of MS Excel.

1. SUM

The equals sign, =, is utilized in all Microsoft Excel formulae, along with a text tag expressing the formula you want Microsoft Excel to perform.

In MS Excel, the SUM formula is one of the most used formulae for finding the sum or total of two or more numbers in a spreadsheet.

To use the SUM formula, enter the numbers you wish to add together in the format =SUM (value 1, value 2, and so on).

Real numbers or the value of a specific cell in your spreadsheet may be entered into the SUM function.

Write the following formula in a cell to determine the SUM of 30 and 80, for example, =SUM (40, 80). When you hit "Enter," the cell displays the sum of the two numbers: 120.

Write the following formula in a cell to get the total values in B2 and B11, for example, =SUM (B2, B11). The cell will compute the sum of the integers in cells B2 and B11 when you hit "Enter." If neither cell has any numbers, the formula will yield zero.

Keep in mind that you can get the cumulative sum of an integer list using Microsoft Excel. To determine the total numbers in cells B2 through B11, use the following formula in a spreadsheet cell: =TOTAL (B2:B11). There is a colon instead of a comma when you include every cell. Here's how it may look in a Microsoft Excel spreadsheet for a content marketer:

SUM	✕ ✓ fx	=SUM(B2:B11)

	A	B
1	**Source of leads**	**Leads generated**
2	Blog post 1	10
3	Blog post 2	4
4	Blog post 3	2
5	Blog post 4	11
6	Blog post 5	12
7	Blog post 6	6
8	Blog post 7	8
9	Blog post 8	17
10	Blog post 9	3
11	Blog post 10	8
12		=SUM(B2:B11)
13		

2. The Average

Simple averages of data should come to mind when using the AVERAGE function.

=AVERAGE (num1, [num2],)

SUM	✕ ✓ fx	=AVERAGE(B2:B12)

	A	B
1	**Country**	**Population**
2	China	1,389,618,778
3	India	1,311,559,204
4	USA	331,883,986
5	Indonesia	264,935,824
6	Pakistan	210,797,836
7	Brazil	210,301,591
8	Nigeria	208,679,114
9	Bangladesh	161,062,905
10	Russia	141,944,641
11	Mexico	127,318,112
12	**Average**	=AVERAGE(B2:B12)
13		

3. COUNT

This counts the number of cells within a range that solely contains numeric values. It is written as

=COUNT (1st value, [2nd value],)

Example:

COUNT (B: B) – Counts all numerical values in column B. To count rows, you must change the range within the calculation.

COUNT (B1:D1) – It now counts rows within the given range.

4. COUNTA

It counts all cells in a range, but the type of data in the cell is ignored. Unlike COUNT, which only counts numeric, this function also counts strings, empty strings, dates, logical values, times, text, and errors.

=COUNTA (1st value, [2nd value2] ....etc.)

Example:

COUNTA (C13:C2) However, unlike COUNT, you can't count rows using the same algorithm. COUNTA (H2:C2), for example, will count the columns C to H if you change the selection within the brackets.

SUM		f_x	=COUNTA(B2:B13)	
	A	**B**	**C**	
1	**Country**	**Population**		
2	China	1,389,618,778		
3	India	1,311,559,204		
4	USA	331,883,986		
5	Indonesia	264,935,824		
6	Pakistan	210,797,836		
7		**Empty**	**Cont all values**	
8	Brazil	210,301,591		
9	Nigeria	208,679,114		
10			**ONLY Skips empty cells**	
11	Bangladesh	161,062,905		
12	Russia	141,944,641		
13	Mexico	127,318,112		
14	**COUNTA**	=COUNTA(B2:B13)	**Output = 11**	
15				

5. IF Statement

This sorts data according to certain rules. This formula includes formulae and functions.

=IF(logical test, [value if true], [value if false])

Example:

=IF(D3<C3, 'TRUE,' 'FALSE') =IF(D3C3, 'TRUE,' 'FALSE') – If the value at C3 is smaller than the value at D3, the condition is true. If the reasoning is correct, set the cell value to TRUE; otherwise, set it to FALSE.

=IF(SUM(F10:F1) > SUM(G10:G1 – A complicated IF logic example. It adds F1 to F10 and G1 to G10 first, then compares the results. When the total of F1 to G10 exceeds the summation of G1 to G10, the cell's value becomes equal to F1 to F10. Otherwise, the SUM of F1 through F10 is calculated.

	X	✓	*fx*	IF=(B2>C2,TRUE,FALSE)	

	A	B	C	D
1	Country	Population	Average Population	Greater than average?
2	China	1,389,618,778	435,810,199	TRUE
3	India	1,311,559,204	435,810,199	TRUE
4	USA	331,883,986	435,810,199	FALSE
5	Indonesia	264,935,824	435,810,199	FALSE
6	Pakistan	210,797,836	435,810,199	FALSE
7	Brazil	210,301,591	435,810,199	FALSE
8	Nigeria	208,679,114	435,810,199	FALSE
9	Bangladesh	161,062,905	435,810,199	FALSE
10	Russia	141,944,641	435,810,199	FALSE
11	Mexico	127,318,112	435,810,199	FALSE
12				

6. TRIM

It is possible to prevent disorganized areas from interfering with your daily activities by using the TRIM feature. That there are no open slots is ensured by this method. When TRIM is used, it only affects a single cell instead of other activities that may affect a group of cells. Therefore, it has the issue of reproducing data on your spreadsheet, which is a disadvantage.

=TRIM(text)

For Instance:

TRIM(A2) – extract empty spaces from cell A2's value.

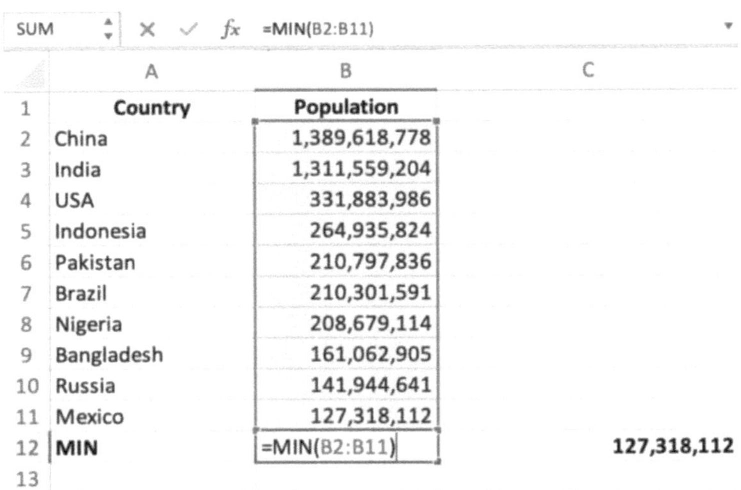

7. MAXIMUM AND MINIMUM

The maximum and minimum functions assist in determining the maximum and minimum values within a series of values.

MINIMUM

=MIN(value1, [value2],…)

MAXIMUM

=MAX(integer1, [interger2],…)

	A	B	C
	Country	Population	
1	**Country**	**Population**	
2	China	1,389,618,778	
3	India	1,311,559,204	
4	USA	331,883,986	
5	Indonesia	264,935,824	
6	Pakistan	210,797,836	
7	Brazil	210,301,591	
8	Nigeria	208,679,114	
9	Bangladesh	161,062,905	
10	Russia	141,944,641	
11	Mexico	127,318,112	
12	**MAX**	=MAX(B2:B11)	1,389,618,778
13			

Formula bar: fx =MAX(B2:B11)

8. Percentage

Type =A1/B1 into the cells you wish to find a percentage in to utilize the percentage formula in Excel Spreadsheets. To convert a decimal number to a %, select the cell, go to the Home tab, and choose "Percentage" from the digits menu.

Although Microsoft Excel doesn't have a "formula" for percentages, it does make it easy to convert the value of any cell to a %, so you don't have to waste time measuring and reentering the numbers.

The particular option for converting the value of a cell to a percentage may be found on Microsoft Excel's Home tab. Choose Conditional Formatting from the drop-down menu next to this column, then highlight the cell(s) you wish to convert to a percent (this menu tab might say "General" first).

Then choose "Percentage" from the drop-down menu that appears. Each cell you've marked will have its meaning transformed to a percentage. You will find it a little farther down the page.

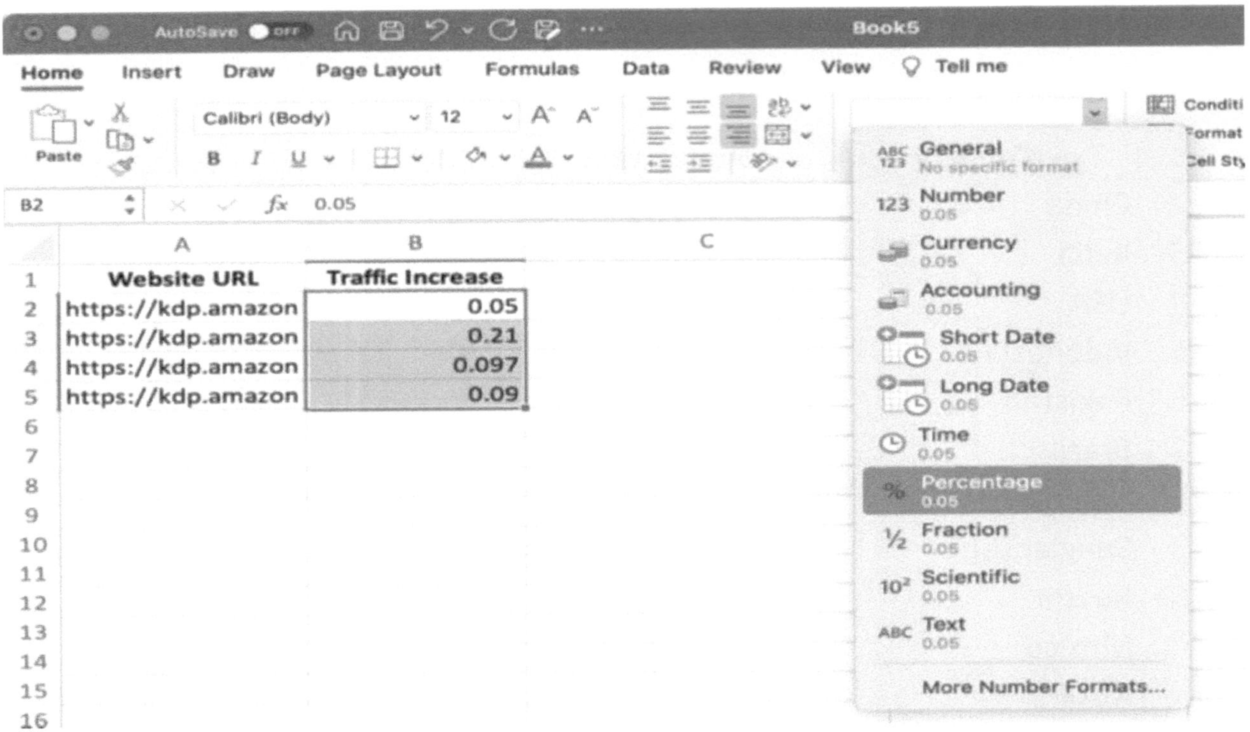

Remember that if you use other formulae to produce new numbers, such as the division formula (notated =A1/B1), the results will default to decimals. Before or after applying this method, select the cells and change their format to "Percentage" using the home tab, as seen above.

9. Subtraction

To run the subtraction algorithm in Microsoft Excel, enter the cells you want to subtract in the format =SUM (A1, -B1). You may use the SUM formula to subtract it by putting a negative sign directly before the cell you're removing. For example, if A1 is 10 and B1 is 6, =SUM(A1, -B1) produces 4 instead of 10 + -6.

In MS Excel, there is no formula for subtractions that involve fractions, but that does not mean that it can't be done. There are two methods for removing particular values (or inside cells).

	A	B	C
	Value 1	Value 2	Results
2	75	85	10
3			

=SUM was used as a formula. In the layout =SUM(A1, -B1), enter the cells you wish to subtract, with the minus sign (denoted by a hyphen) directly before the cell whose value you want to remove. Enter to find the distance between the two parenthesis cells. Take a look at the image above to get a sense of how this works.

10. Multiplication

Insert the cells for multiplying in Microsoft Excel in the format =A1*B1 to run the multiplication formula. In this formula, an asterisk is used to multiply cell A1 by cell B1. If A1 is 10 and B1 is 6, for example, the result of =A1*B1 is 60.

You could think that multiplying values in MS Excel has a formula or that the "x" character signifies multiple multiplied values.

Using an asterisk — * — is all it takes.

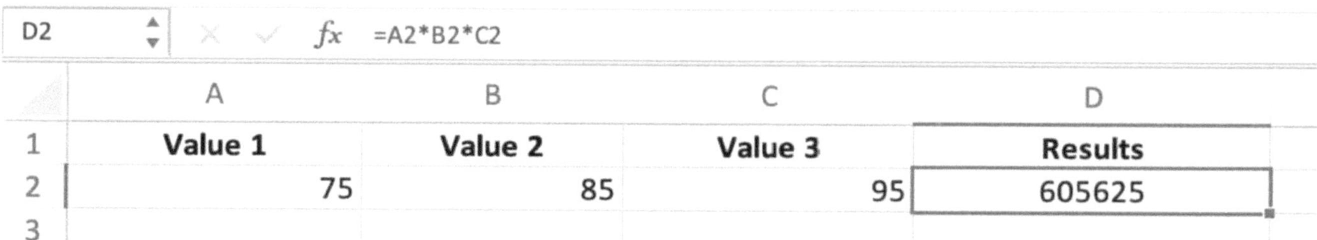

Mark an empty cell in an MS Excel spreadsheet to multiply two or more numbers. Then, in the format =A1*B1*C1..., put the numbers or cells you want to multiply together in the format =A1*B1*C1... The asterisk would effectively double each meaning in the calculation.

Press Enter to return your preferred item. To show how this works, check the screenshot above.

11. Division

In MS Excel, put =F1/G1 into the cells you wish to divide to utilize the division formula. The forward slash, "/," splits cell F1 by cell G1. For example, if F1 is 10 and G1 is 20, =F1/G1 returns 0.5 as a decimal number.

The division is one of the most fundamental functions in Microsoft Excel. To do so, open a new cell and write "=," followed by the two (or more) values you wish to divide, separated by a forward dash, "/." The result should be in the format =B2/A2, as seen in the image below.

	A	B	C
			fx =B2/A2
1	**Value 1**	**Value 2**	**Results**
2	75	85	1,133333333
3			

When you hit Enter, the highlighted cell will display your selected quotient.

12. DATE TIME

The MS Excel DATE formula is DATE =DATE (year, month, day). This formula will provide a date that matches the data in the brackets and values from other cells. For example, if A1 is 2018, B1 is 7, and C1 is 11, =DATE(A1,B1,C1) returns 7/11/2018.

It might be tough to input dates into the cells of a Microsoft Excel database at times. Fortunately, formatting dates is easy using a simple formula. This formula can be used in two different ways:

To make dates, use a series of cell values. Select an empty cell, enter "=DATE," and then put the values of the cells that make up your chosen date in parentheses, starting with the year, month number, and ending with the day. DATE= (year, month, day). To show how this works, check the screenshot below.

Set a date for today automatically. Select an empty cell and enter =DATE(YEAR(TODAY()), MONTH(TODAY()), DAY(TODAY()) in it. The most recent date in your MS Excel spreadsheet will be returned if you click enter.

	A	B	C	D
			fx =DATE(A4; B4; C4)	
1	**Year**	**Month**	**Day**	**Date**
2	2018	12	2	02/02/18
3	2018	2	18	18/02/18
4	2018	7	11	11/07/18
5				

Assume your Microsoft Excel program is set up differently. In any scenario of utilizing the date formula in Microsoft Excel, your returned date must be in the format "mm/dd/yy."

13. Match

To use the MATCH formula in Microsoft Excel, first select a list. Then type the string to be matched. If the result is an empty string, the match function will return an error. This error indicates that no match was found. If your data isn't sorted in the order you entered it, then type a search in the first column of the data set. The second column will return the position of the value matched by the MATCH function.

When using the MS Excel MATCH formula, you can search for a specific value in a column. If a value is present in cell G2, the MATCH formula will return that value in the range A2 to A9. For a specific array, you can use the INDEX function, which returns a single value in a range by comparing the position of that value against the number in the column. In addition, the INDEX formula takes into account the relative row number.

To check the position for 62:

A9 fx =MATCH(62, A1:A7, 0)

	A	B	C	D	E
1	540				
2	23				
3	45				
4	62				
5	45				
6	34				
7	72				
8					
9	4				

Checking the position for 69 will bring error displayed as #N/A:

There are three main ways to use the Match Formula in MS Excel. The first is to use a 'number' as the lookup value. This allows you to easily search for numbers or text within a cell. The second method is to use a 'text' value, which works the same way as a regular cell reference. These two methods are both used to search for strings in documents and spreadsheets. The first method allows you to specify the match type, which is also known as 'text,' and the second approach uses a "reference" to return the value.

Another way to use the Match Function in MS Excel is by creating a lookup table. You can also use the INDEX function to locate specific values within a list. The INDEX function returns the value in a particular column and gives you its reference in the same position in the other column. To create a lookup table in MS Excel, use the "JK002" as the first parameter. Using the INDEX function will return a value with the same name as the number in column A.

14. How to Use the VLOOKUP Function in MS Excel

The VLOOKUP function in MS Excel allows you to look up specific information about a particular item. This feature allows you to enter the details of a particular item, such as a specific grade, and find out if that grade has already been assigned to another item. VLOOKUP can also be used to look up a single item from an inventory list. The following steps will guide you through the process. If you are not familiar with VLOOKUP, you can use a short video to get an overview.

First, identify the column you'd like to fill in. Next, select the Functions tab and choose VLOOKUP. You can then type the formula into the highlighted cell. In addition, you can type the lookup value and column number into the formula. Once you've done this, click the "Done" button. This will populate the first cell. You can also check the value of your VLOOKUP formula by clicking the tiny square on the bottom right corner of the cell.

When using VLOOKUP, you should be very careful with your input value. The lookup value can be a number or a text string. If it's a number, you don't need to use quotes; the default value is TRUE. The range_lookup parameter specifies whether the lookup value must be exact or approximate. If it's not, you can specify an approximate match.

E2 fx =VLOOKUP(E1, A2:B7, 2, FALSE)

	A	B	C	D	E	F
1	**Animal**	**Speed(mph)**		**Animal**	Antelope	
2	Cheetah	70		**Speed**	61	
3	Zebra	59				
4	Antelope	61				
5	Lion	50				
6	Elk	45				
7	Coyote	43				
8						

15. Financial Formulas

Financial formulas calculate financial transactions using money values, such as interest rates and percentages. To learn how to write financial formulas in Excel, you will need to know how to use some financial formulas in formulas that operate with these values.

16. How to Use the Random Numbers Generator in Microsoft Excel

This section will show you how to use the Random numbers generator in Microsoft Excel to generate random numbers for your data. This is an analytics tool that you can use to find out patterns. Its various options include a lower and an upper limit, step, and repetition rate for both values and sequence. You can even sort the results using a column. In the end, the sum of probabilities should equal one. But it's not as simple as that. There are more sophisticated options for Excel.

First, choose the range you wish to use to generate random numbers. You can either select a range of cells or specify a pre-selected range. If you don't specify a range, Excel will generate a new one. If you choose a specific range, the generated data will overwrite the existing data. Choose the New Worksheet Ply option if you want to insert a new worksheet within the current workbook. You can then paste the random data into cell A1 in the first sheet. After completing this step, press the OK button.

You can use the formula as:

=rand() or

=randbetween(minimum_value,max_value)

Once you have created the ranges, you can use the formula to generate random numbers. To find out how many numbers are in each category, enter the formula for rounddown in cell E1. After the formula, you should see a chart with a normal distribution. Ideally, this chart will resemble a bell shape.

1.56 Building Basic Formulas

1.56.1 Adding Array Formulas in MS Excel
An array formula is a method that can perform several calculations on multiple items in an array. An array is a collection of data in a column or row or a collection of data in a combination of columns and rows. Array formulas may give several results or simply one. As you may know, the combination of multiple keys CTRL + SHIFT + ENTER converts an ordinary equation into an array formula.

Array formulas may be utilized to do complex tasks like:

1. Quickly create sample datasets.

2. Count the number of letters in a group of cells.

3. Only include numbers that meet particular requirements, such as those in the lower half of a range or ones that fall between two lines.

4. In a collection of numbers, add up all Nth values.

There are many uses for Array Formulas in MS Excel. You can return the Nth largest or smallest value from a set, or return a specified number of either the smallest or the largest numbers. Arrays can also count and ignore errors. They can even calculate based on IF and conditional logic. Adding Array Formulas to MS Excel is easy, and the following steps will walk you through the process.

First, you must select the cells where the array formula will be used. These cells are usually called Array Block or Array Range. This is because you cannot edit individual cells within the array formula. Likewise, you cannot change the cell references within the array formula. You must specify a number of rows for the cell ranges where the array formula will be placed. The number of rows must be the same for all the ranges so that the temporary arrays will have the same length.

Once you have the data in the range, you can add an array formula. An array formula consists of a series of numbers that can be added together to produce a number. An array formula is an expression in Excel that encloses the values within curly braces. You can view the resulting sum in the formula bar by pressing F9 and selecting the arguments. If you need a formula to calculate the number of values in an array, then use the same procedure as above.

SUM	✕ ✓	fx	=SUM(B2:B8*C2:C8)

	A	B	C	D
1	Shopping List Items		Price per item	
2	Mangoes	40	$ 11.00	
3	Grapes	23	$ 7.00	
4	Biscuits	45	$ 1.00	
5	Exercise books	62	$ 10.00	
6	Cups	45	$ 8.00	
7	Pencils	34	$ 4.00	
8	Beads	72	$ 2.00	
9				
10	Total Cost		C2:C8)	

C10			fx	=SUM(B2:B8*C2:C8)

	A	B	C	D
1	Shopping List	Items	Price per item	
2	Mangoes	40	$ 11.00	
3	Grapes	23	$ 7.00	
4	Biscuits	45	$ 1.00	
5	Exercise books	62	$ 10.00	
6	Cups	45	$ 8.00	
7	Pencils	34	$ 4.00	
8	Beads	72	$ 2.00	
9				
10	Total Cost		$ 1,906.00	

1.56.2 APPLYING NAME ATTRIBUTES IN RANGE OPERATIONS

Giving names to ranges of cell help to point to them when executing formatting or mathematical operations.

However, there are certain key requirements for naming named ranges in Excel that you should be aware of before you begin:

1. There are no spaces allowed in names. Instead of using a space, you might use an underscore character (such as Annual_Total).

2. You may name the range with any combination of alphabets and digits, but it must begin using a letter symbol. A number cannot begin a name.

3. Except for underscores and periods, no other symbols are permitted.

4. Although names are restricted to 255 characters, it is best to make them as brief as possible while still being relevant and clear.

Excel also keeps a few names in reserve for internal use. Although it is possible to construct names that override Excel's internal names, this is something you should avoid.

HOW TO ASSIGN NAMES TO RANGES

Using the Name Box

- Highlight the ranges to be named

- Navigate to the box for names beside the formula bar and type in your desired name

- This name is applied to the entire workbook for that cell range.

Employing the Dialogue Box for Assigning New Range Names

- To restrict range names to only a particular worksheet, use this option to define a range name in the **Formula** bar.

- First, select the cell range to be named and navigate to the option to define a name in the **Formula** bar

- In the dialogue box that appears for new names, enter an appropriate name and set a restriction level for the name

- Select the Ok button

Using the Dialogue Box for Selection

- Highlight the whole data you have on your worksheet

- Navigate to the option to create a selection in the **Formula** bar

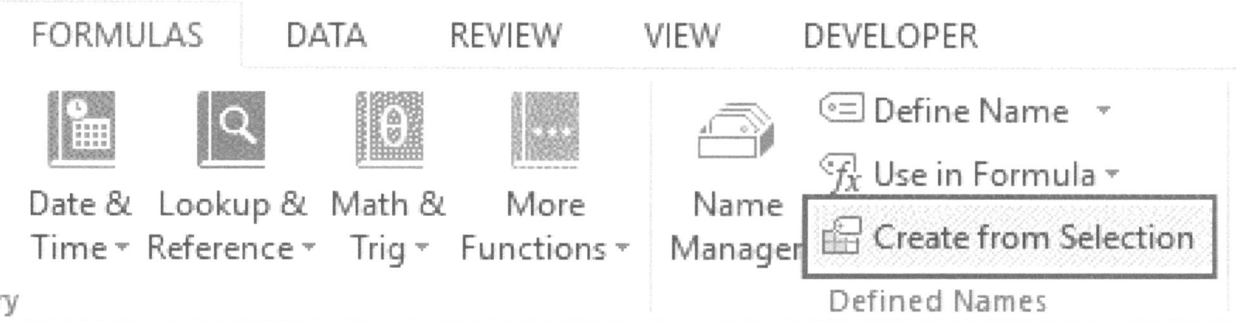

- When the dialogue box for "**Create Names from Selection**" is opened, select where a name should be chosen from in the highlighted data

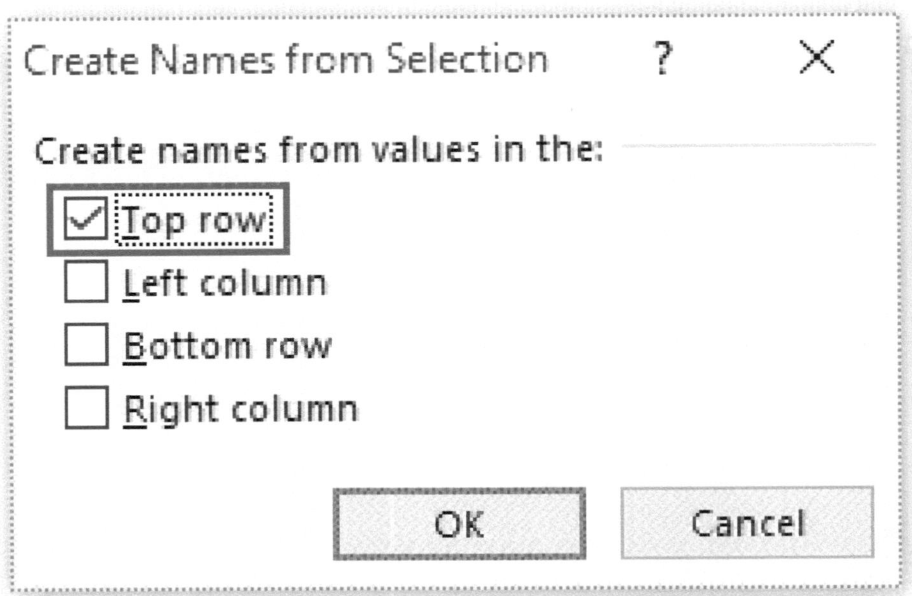

This technique chooses names for ranges from what you have on your worksheet. Range names do not support blank spaces; they are usually replaced with underscores.

WORKING WITH NAMES IN RANGES

In case you have a lot of range names already created in your worksheet, these names can be edited and managed using the **Manager for Names** in the option for defined names found in the **Formula** tab. Keyboard keys **Ctrl + F3** can also be used to access this **Manager.**

While in this Manager, you can select to add new names, edit existing names, or even delete them. Select the OK button to save all changes.

1.56.3 Fixing circular reference errors
Understand the problem: A pop-up window with a warning about a "circular reference" appears. Cyclical reference refers to the fact that a cell refers to itself, resulting in a circular process. This may arise, for example, if a cell in which you wish to display the result of a calculation appears within the calculation itself, e.g. =TOTAL(A1:A10). You want to show the result in cell A1.

How to solve the problem: You have to select another cell to display the result or check whether cells refer to themselves.

A circular reference mistake arises when a formula refers to a cell that currently has it, either explicitly or implicitly. Consequently, the formula dynamically adjusts the previously acquired result, resulting in this sort of mistake. When your worksheet has a circular reference, the automated computation will not be executed.

Alternatively, you'll have to utilize Excel's error checker to figure out where the circular references are and then eliminate them. When you don't do so, each cell will be computed in the circular reference with the preceding iteration's findings. Remember that iterating involves continuing the recompilation procedure until it satisfies a set of numerical requirements.

There are ways to solve this issue. You can activate the iterative calculation function. Select File > Options > Formulas > Tick the box on Enable iterative calculation. You can also move the formula to another cell manually. To find the cell causing the issue, use the Check for Error option.

MS Excel Logical Functions

Logical functions in MS Excel allow you to perform calculations based on a logical value. A logical value that returns TRUE is called a TRUE logical function, and the converse happens if the corresponding value is FALSE.

Logical functions in Excel combine conditional tests with boolean operators to make decisions about data sets. These tests check multiple conditions and return a value corresponding to the first one that evaluates TRUE. However, if the first condition is false, the function will return a different value. If all of the arguments produce a TRUE, the AND function will return a TRUE value. This function can be used to test multiple variables at once and is extremely useful for evaluating data sets.

Here are some common logical functions:

AND Function

You can use the AND function whenever you want to evaluate multiple conditions in Excel. It only returns TRUE if all of the supplied conditions are met. If all conditions are true in Microsoft Excel, the AND function gives TRUE. If any of the conditions are false, it returns FALSE. The AND function is an Excel built-in function that is classified as a Logical Function.

Syntax: AND (condition1, [condition2], ...)

Example:

D1		f_x	=AND(A1>10, A1<40)		
	A	B	C	D	E	F
1	30			TRUE		
2	www.techonthenet.com					
3						
4						
5						
6						

The following AND samples would be returned based on the Excel spreadsheet above:

A1>10, A1>40) =AND (A1>10, A1>40)

TRUE is the outcome.

IF Function

The Excel IF Function is an in-built function that is classified as a Logical Function and it is generally used when examining a condition, returning a value if TRUE or FALSE. If the condition is TRUE, the IF function in MS Excel returns one value, and if the condition is FALSE, it gives another value.

Syntax: IF (condition, value if true, [value if false])

Example:

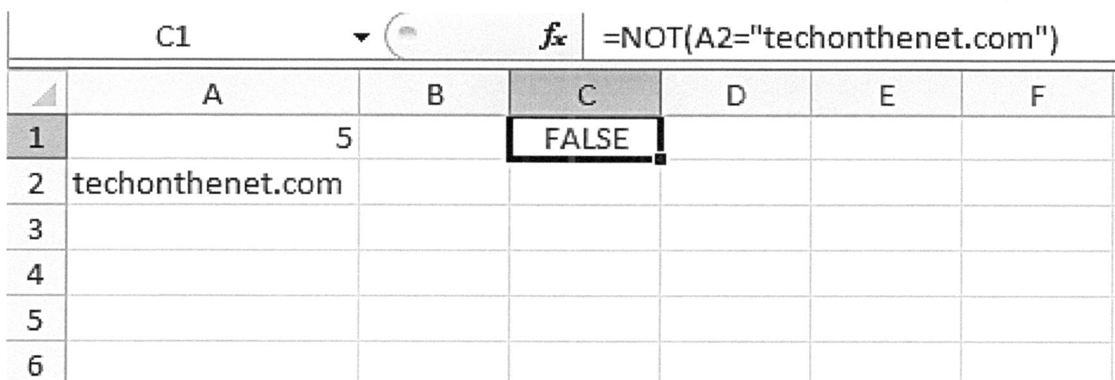

=IF (B2<10, "Reorder", "") "Reorder" is the result.

NOT Function

The NOT function is an Excel built-in function that is classified as a Logical Function. If you wish to reverse a value of the logical argument (TRUE/FALSE), you can use the NOT function in Excel. The NOT function in MS Excel returns the logical value in reverse.

Syntax: NOT (logical value)

Example:

=NOT (A2="techonthenet.com") Result is FALSE

OR

The OR function is an Excel built-in function that is classified as a Logical Function. You can use the OR function whenever you want to evaluate multiple conditions in Excel. If some of the given conditions are true, it returns TRUE. If the conditions are true, the Microsoft Excel OR function gives TRUE. Otherwise, FALSE is returned.

Syntax: OR (condition1, [condition2, ... condition_n])

Example:

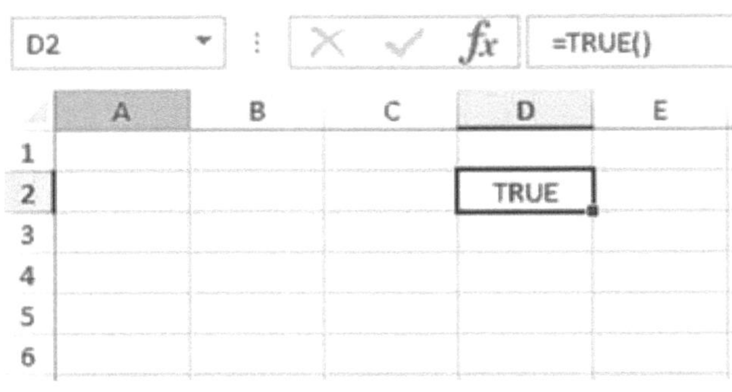

=OR (A1=10, A1=40) FALSE is the outcome.

TRUE

The TRUE function in Excel is a logical function that comes with the software. The TRUE function in Excel delivers TRUE as a logical value. It does not accept any arguments as input.

Syntax: TRUE ( )

Example:

=TRUE () Result is TRUE.

FALSE

The FALSE function is an Excel built-in function that is classified as a Logical Function. The FALSE function in MS Excel returns a logical value of FALSE. It does not accept any arguments as input.

Syntax: FALSE ( )

Example:

=FALSE () Result is FALSE

IFERROR

The IFERROR function in MS Excel is best for formulas that result in an error. If the formula produces an error, you can select a value to display. If a formula fails, the IFERROR function in MS Excel returns an alternative value. It will look for #N/A, #REF!, #NAME?, #DIV/o!, #VALUE!, #NUM!, or #NULL problems. It is an Excel built-in function that is classified as a Logical Function.

Syntax: IFERROR (formula, alternate_value)

Example:

	A	B	C	D	E
1				Price/Unit	
2	Cost	Quantity		Formula Result	IFERROR Result
3	$12.50	0		#DIV/0!	$0.00
4	$3.00	6		$0.50	$0.50
5	$7.00	10		$0.70	$0.70
6	$9.75	0		#DIV/0!	$0.00
7	$8.00	30		$0.27	$0.27
8					

It produces 0 (the alternate value). Error:

=IFERROR (A3/B3,0) 0 is a result

IFNA

If a formula returns a #N/A error, the Microsoft Excel IFNA function returns back a substitute value. The IFNA function is an Excel built-in function that is classified as a Logical Function.

Syntax: IFNA (formula, alternate value)

Example:

When utilizing functions that potentially return #N/A error, such as VLOOKUP, HLOOKUP, or LOOKUP, the IFNA function comes in handy. The IFNA function can return a different result in some circumstances instead of #N/A error code.

Column F of the Excel spreadsheet above has a VLOOKUP algorithm for determining the Unit Price for the product name in column E.

When the VLOOKUP function fails, Column G utilizes the IFNA function to return back an alternate value of 0.

Because the VLOOKUP function VLOOKUP (E3,$A$3:$C$7,2, FALSE) resulted in #N/A error, the IFNA equation in G3 cell would return back a value of 0 (i.e., the alternate value):

| G3 | | | f_x | =IFNA(VLOOKUP(E3,$A$3:$C$7,2,FALSE),0) | | |

	A	B	C	D	E	F	G	H
1						Unit Price		
2	Product	Unit Price	Quantity		Product	Formula Result	IFNA Result	
3	Apples	$14.00	12		Watermelons	#N/A	$0.00	
4	Oranges	$9.80	10		Apples	$14.00	$14.00	
5	Bananas	$34.80	5					
6	Pears	$18.60	9					
7	Grapes	$42.30	40					
8								

=IFNA (VLOOKUP (E3,$A$3:$C$7,2,FALSE),0)

The result is $0.00

IFS

The IFS function is an Excel built-in function that is classified as a Logical Function. This function can be used when you wish to test numerous conditions at once to produce a response based on the results. This is advantageous since it eliminates the need for large, nested IF formulae that can be confusing. The IFS function in MS Excel allows you to define several IF conditions in a single function call.

Syntax: IFS (condition1, return1 [,condition2, return2] ... [,condition127, return127])

Example:

C2				f_x	=IFS(A2="Apple","Fruit",A2="Potato","Veg", A2="Steak","Meat")

	A	B	C	D	E	F
1	Item		IFS Result	IFS Result (with ELSE)		
2	Apple		Fruit	Fruit		
3	Potato		Veg	Veg		
4	Steak		Meat	Meat		
5	Coffee		#N/A	Misc		
6						

Result is "Fruit"

MS Excel Lookup and Text's Functions

It is possible to turn integers into text within an Excel spreadsheet by using the TEXT Function. In its most basic form, the function turns a numeric number into a text string of specified length. TEXT is a feature that is present in all versions of the Excel spreadsheet software.

When is the TEXT function in Excel required?

It is necessary to utilize the TEXT function in the following situations:

- When we need dates to be displayed in a certain format;

- When we want numbers to be presented in a specific format or a more understandable manner;

- In situations where we need to blend numerical data with text or characters.

Left()

Left is a function that can be used to extract the characters that are on the left-hand side of a string. The left function is equal to the text plus the number of characters.

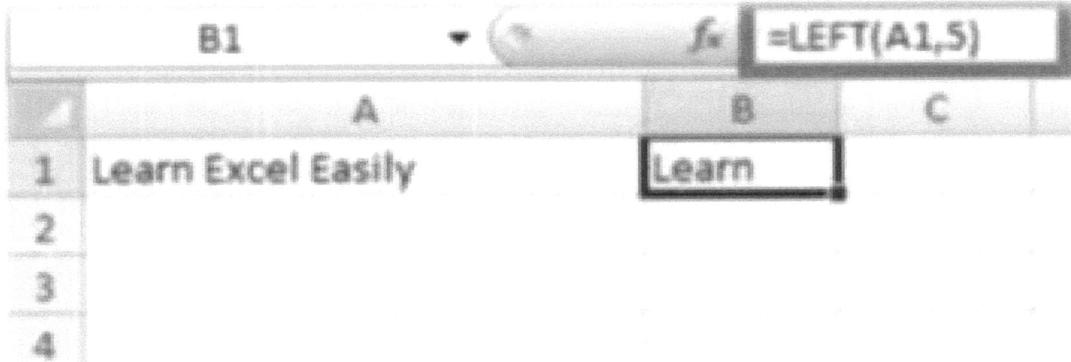

Similarly, you can use the Right function to retrieve the string's rightmost characters.

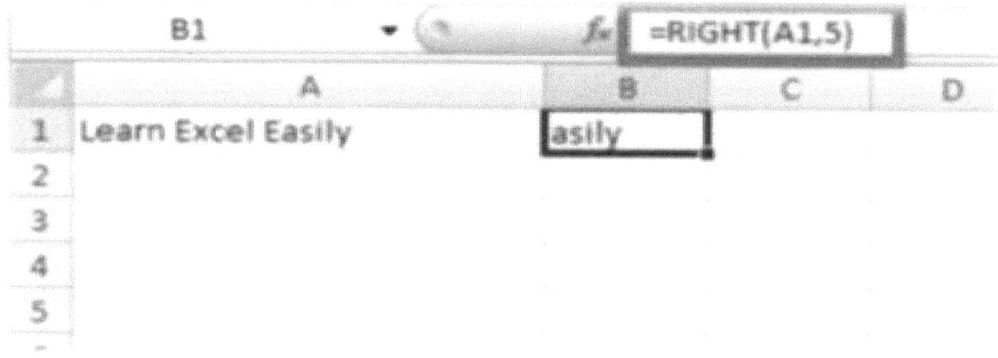

Mid ()

The Mid function in Excel is used to pull characters from the middle of a string. = MID(text, first character, number of characters)

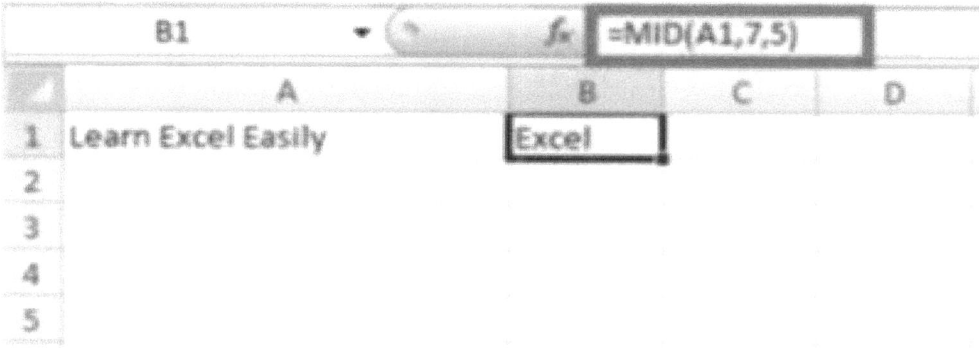

Find ()

The Find function in Microsoft Excel is used to locate certain characters within a string of characters. = FIND(find text, within text, [start num]).

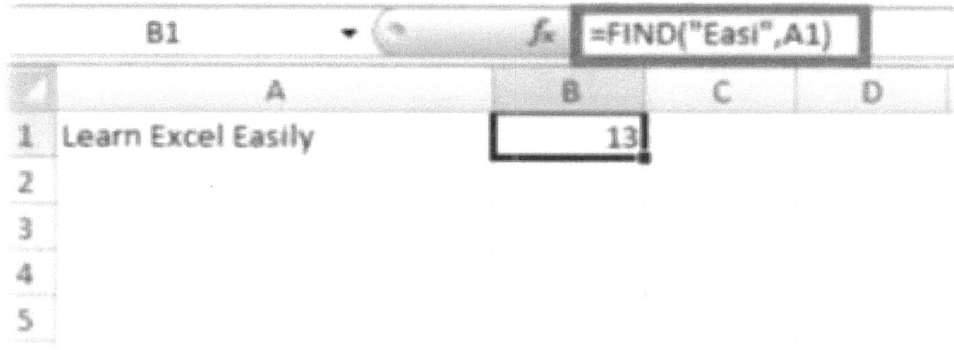

Rept ()

It is possible to repeat a string of text in Excel a given number of times using the Rept function.
=REPT(Text, number of times)

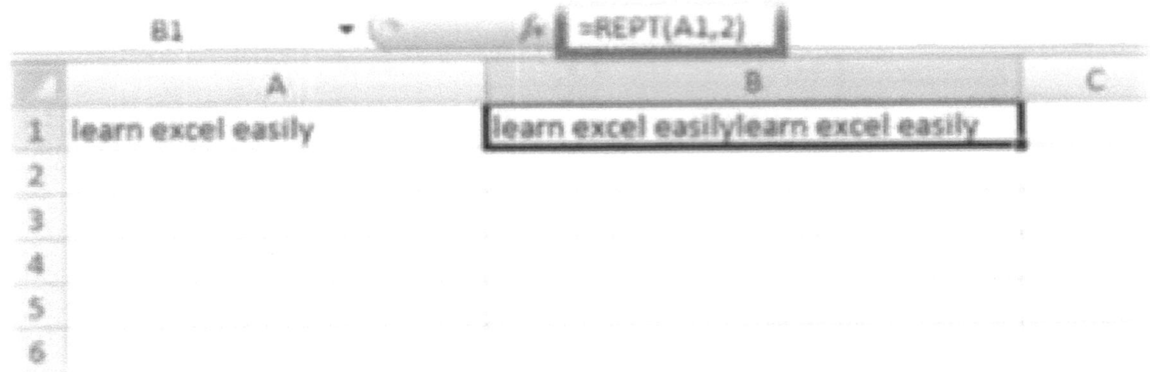

COLUMN Function

When you need to find the column number of a certain cell in Excel, use the COLUMN function.

COLUMNS Function

It can determine the number with columns in a range or array. It gives you a number that measures the total columns in the range or array you specified.

HLOOKUP Function

The HLOOKUP function in Excel is best used when you're seeking a similar data point in such a row. Once you've found it, you want to go down the column and get a certain value from the cell that's several rows just below upper row.

INDIRECT Function

If one has text references and wishes to acquire the values through them, you can use the INDIRECT function in Excel. It returns the text string's provided reference.

MATCH Function

You can use the MATCH function in Excel to get the position relative or even a lookup a given value in a particular array or list. It produces a number indicating the lookup value's location in the given array.

VLOOKUP Function

The VLOOKUP function in Excel is best used when you're seeking a similar data point within a given column. Once you've found it, you move towards the right section within this row and get a particular value from just a cell that's a specified feature vector towards the right.

TEXTJOIN

The TEXTJOIN function in MS Excel lets you join two or more strings together, you can separate each of the values using a delimiter. The TEXTJOIN function is a worksheet function that you can use in a formula in a worksheet cell.

Syntax:

TEXTJOIN (delimiter, ignore empty, text1, [text2,... text n])

Example:

E2				f_x	=TEXTJOIN(",",TRUE,A2,B2,C2,D2)	

	A	B	C	D	E	F
1	Text1	Text2	Text3	Text4	Result	
2	A	B	C	D	A,B,C,D	
3	1	2	3	4	1,2,3,4	
4	Tech	On	The	Net	Tech,On,The,Net	
5	alpha	bet			alpha,bet	
6						
7						

The following TEXTJOIN instances would be returned relying on the Excel spreadsheet above:

The result is "A,B,C,D"

TRIM

The TRIM function is an Excel built-in function that is classified as a Text Function. It returns a text value that has the leading and following spaces removed. This function is used to reduce unwanted spaces between words in a string.

Syntax: TRIM (text)

Example:

	A	B	C	D	E
1	Tech on the Net		Tech on the Net		
2	1234				
3	alphabet soup				
4	www.techonthenet.com				
5					

=TRIM (A1) Result is "Tech on the Net"

LEN

The LEN function in MS Excel returns the length of the provided string. The LEN function is an Excel built-in function that is classified as a String/Text Function. It can be used as a worksheet equation (WS) and a VBA formula (VBA) in Excel.

Syntax: LEN (text)

A string's length can be determined using the Len function in Excel, which is defined as the total number of characters in the string. LEN is the same as syntax (text)

Please keep in mind that gaps are taken into consideration while determining length. (A1) gives 18

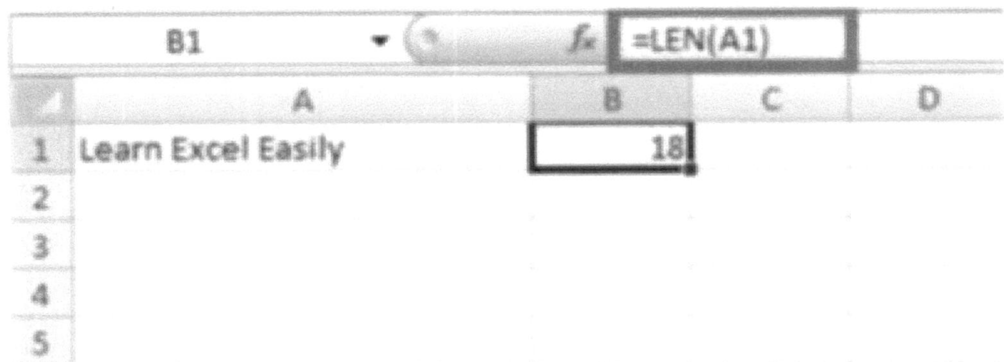

CLEAN

The CLEAN function in MS Excel eliminates any nonprintable characters from a string. The CLEAN function can act as a section of a formula within a cell.

Syntax: CLEAN (text)

Example:

	A	B	C	D	E	F	G
			fx =CLEAN(A1)				
1	▯hi there		hi there				
2	▯this is a test▯▯						
3							
4							
5							
6							

The following CLEAN samples would be returned:

=CLEAN (A1) Result is "hi there."

EXACT

The EXACT function is an Excel built-in function that is classified as a Text Function. It compares different strings and returns TRUE when both values are equal. Otherwise, FALSE will be returned.

Syntax: EXACT (text1, text2)

Example:

	A	B	C	D	E	F	G
			fx =EXACT(A1, A2)				
1	techonthenet.com		FALSE				
2	Techonthenet.com						
3	alphabet						
4	Alphabet						
5	alphabet						
6							

=EXACT (A1, A2) Result is FALSE

PROPER

The PROPER function is an Excel built-in function that is classified as a Text Function. It makes the initial character in each word uppercase and the remainder lowercase. The PROPER function can be used as part of a formula in a worksheet cell.

Syntax: PROPER (text)

Example:

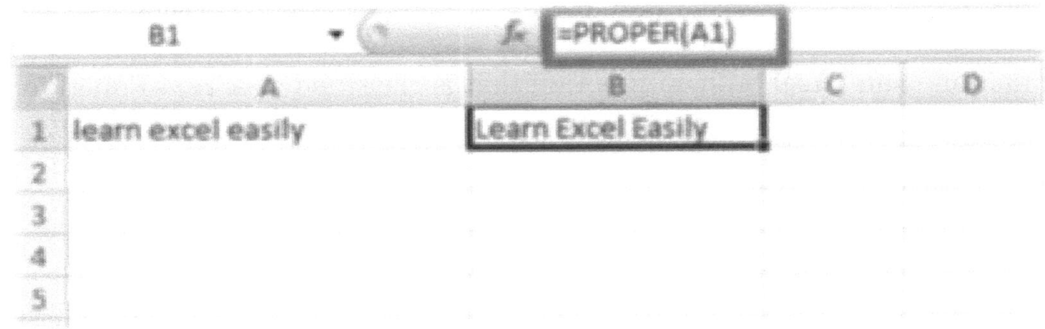

=PROPER (A1) Result is "Alphabet Soup."

REPLACE

It replaces a string's series of characters with a different set of characters.

Syntax: REPLACE (old text, start, number of chars, new text)

Example:

The following REPLACE examples might return based on the Excel worksheet above:

=REPLACE (A1, 1, 5, "Beta") Result is "Betabet Soup."

SUBSTITUTE

The SUBSTITUTE function is an Excel built-in function that is classified as a Text Function. It replaces a set of characters with another set.

Syntax: SUBSTITUTE (text, old text, new text, [nth appearance])

Example:

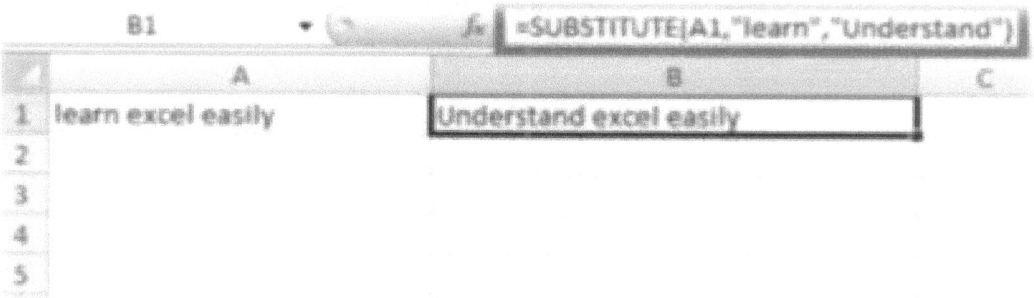

The following SUBSTITUTE examples would be returned:

=SUBSTITUTE (A1, "bet", "con", 1) Result is "Alphacon soup"

CONCATENATE

This function allows you to merge two or more strings. The CONCATENATE can be implemented as a section of a formula.

Syntax: CONCATENATE (text1, [text2,... text n])

Example:

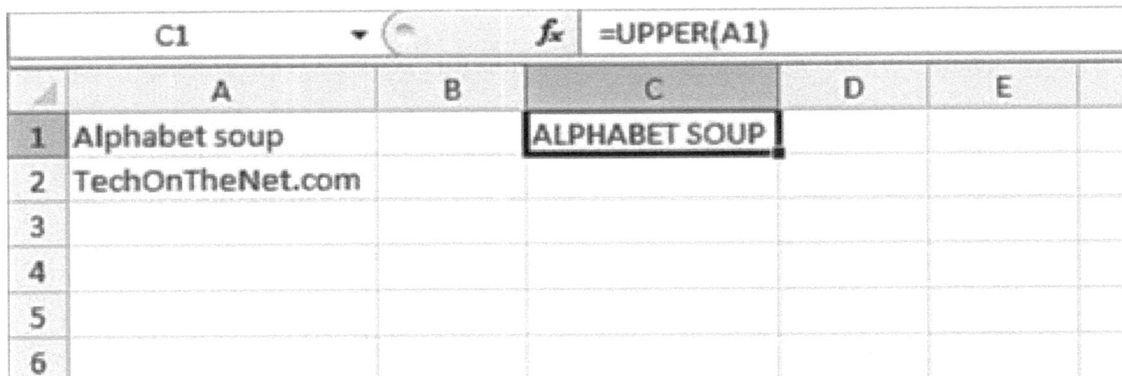

The result is "EFGH"

UPPER

The UPPER function in MS Excel helps to convert text to all uppercase. The UPPER function is part of the Text Functions included in Excel.

Syntax: UPPER (text)

Example: =UPPER (A1)

Result is "ALPHABET SOUP"

LOWER

The LOWER function in MS Excel turns all letters in a string to lowercase. If the string contains any characters that aren't letters, this function does not affect them. The LOWER function is a Text Function that is included in Excel.

Syntax: LOWER (text)

Example:

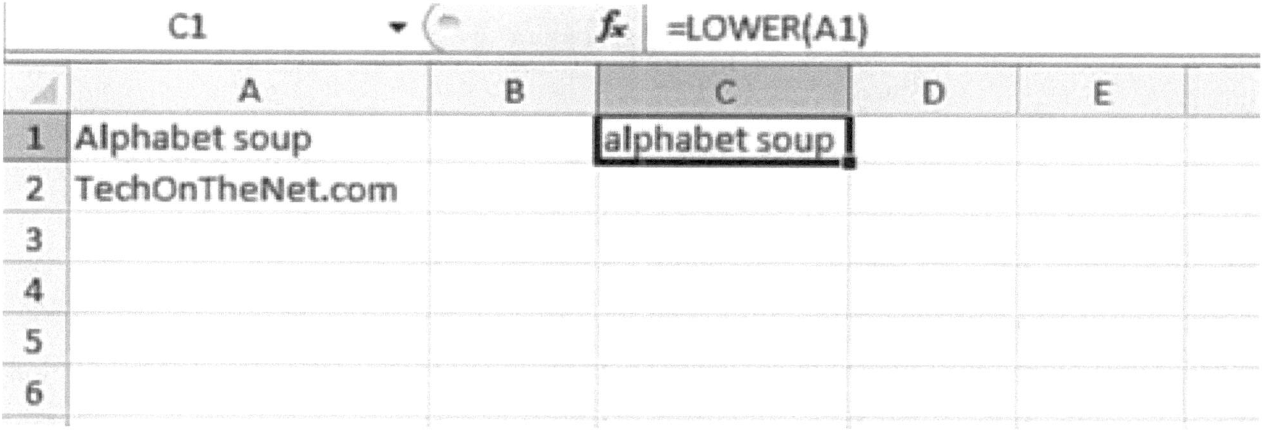

Result: =LOWER (A1)

The result is "alphabet soup"

MS Excel Counting Functions

COUNT is a statistical function in the Microsoft Excel spreadsheet program. In addition to identifying the number of cells containing numbers, this function also assists in determining the number of arguments containing numbers. Additionally, it will count the number of elements in any array that is provided. Excel 2000 was the first version to have it.

When analyzing data, it is helpful for a financial analyst to note the cells that fall within a specific range.

Many people understand the use of the COUNT function in Microsoft which is to count cells. However, there are four separate COUNT functions available, and you may not be aware of the subtle differences between them until now.

Here are some commonly used counting functions:

COUNT

The COUNT function is used to determine the number of cells in a range that contain numerical information. This may be used to determine the number of individual transactions carried out by a household, the number of sales completed by a business, and so on.

Teachers can even use this to track student absences by recording a present student with an alphabetic entry, such as "P," and an absent student with a numeric entry, such as "0." By applying the COUNT function, this teacher can then allow Excel to do the work of tracking how often each student was absent.

To continue our household expenses example from the previous chapter, we will use the worksheet:

	A	B	C	D
1	Date	Spending Type	Amount Spent	Who
2	01/01/2021	Housing	$ 1,200.00	Split
3	01/01/2021	Utilities	$ 432.00	Split
4	01/01/2021	Food	$ 100.00	Lisa
5	03/01/2021	Transportation	$ 20.00	Frank
6	04/01/2021	Other	$ 13.50	Lisa
7	07/01/2021	Other	$ 8.75	Lisa
8	08/01/2021	Food	$ 102.00	Frank
9	08/01/2021	Transportation	$ 25.00	Lisa
10	11/01/2021	Transportation	$ 15.00	Frank
11	14/01/2021	Food	$ 98.25	Lisa
12	14/01/2021	Utilities	$ 65.25	Split
13	17/01/2021	Other	$ 4.90	Frank
14	18/01/2021	Food	$ 6.20	Lisa
15	21/01/2021	Food	$ 121.00	Frank
16	21/01/2021	Other	$ 39.30	Frank
17	23/01/2021	Transportation	$ 30.00	Lisa
18	24/01/2021	Food	$ 11.20	Frank
19	28/01/2021	Food	$ 103.95	Lisa
20	29/01/2021	Other	$ 21.30	Frank
21	31/01/2021	Other	$ 2.80	Frank
22				

To determine the total number of transactions for the month, we can use the function:

=COUNT(C:C)

This function uses the entire C column as the cell range to be counted. If additional expenditure rows are added retrospectively, our COUNT function will automatically update to include them.

COUNTA

The COUNTA function counts all non-empty cells. Therefore, rather than just including numerical data, as the COUNT function does, COUNTA includes numbers, dates, text, logical values, error values, spaces, and so on, as cells which contain data. This is why this function is sometimes referred to as the "COUNT IF not blank" function.

The structure to use COUNTA is as follows.

=COUNTA(value1, value2, …)

With any COUNT-type function, up to 233 additional arguments to be included in the count can be entered inside the parentheses, as long as they are separated by commas.

COUNTIF

The COUNTIF function allows us to set the criteria to filter the information that we wish to count. This can be applied to both numeric and non-numeric information, like the COUNTA function.

The structure for the use of COUNTIF is:

=COUNTIF(range, criteria)

Therefore, if we wanted to know how many household expenditures occurred on the first of January, we could use the function:

=COUNTIF(A:A, "01/01/2021")

Likewise, to count the number of transactions below $20, we might use:

=COUNTIF(C2:C21, "<20")

COUNTBLANK

What if you want to do the opposite and only count the cells that aren't filled in? Then you can use COUNTBLANK.

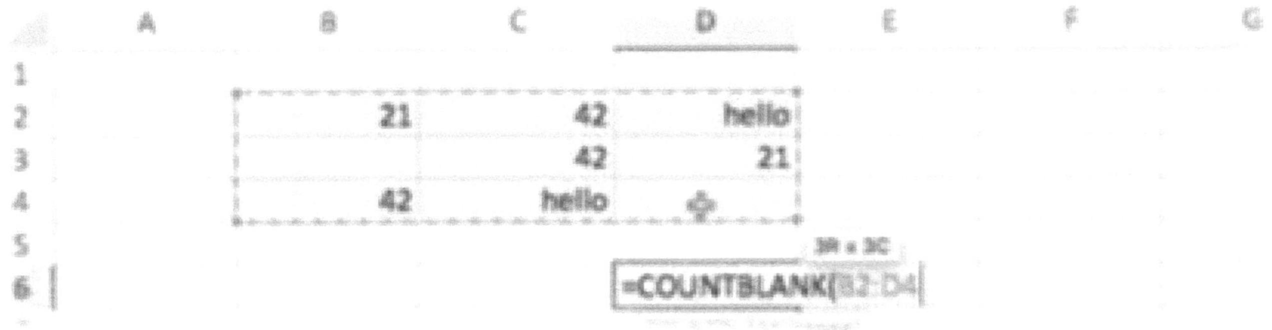

Due to the presence of two blank cells, the outcome is correct.

The COUNTBLANK function in MS Excel counts the number of empty cells in a range.

Syntax: COUNTBLANK (range)

Example:

	A	B	C	D	E	F
				fx	=COUNTBLANK(A1:A4)	
1	www.techonthenet.com			1		
2		32	89			
3			-12			
4	123abc					
5						
6						

=COUNTBLANK (A1:A4) Result is 1

FREQUENCY

The FREQUENCY function in MS Excel returns the frequency with which values appear in a piece of data. It gives you a vertical array of numbers as a result.

Syntax: FREQUENCY (data, intervals)

Example:

	A	B	C	D	E	F
			fx	=FREQUENCY(B2:B10,D2)		
1	Name	Test Score		Intervals		
2	Joanne	80		59		
3	Andrew	75		69		
4	George	90		79		
5	Angela	62		89		
6	Marissa	83				
7	John	55				
8	Henry	76				
9	Amanda	93				
10	Darryl	58				
11						
12	2					

=FREQUENCY (B2:B10, D2) Result is 2

MIN

The MIN function in MS Excel produces the smallest value from a set of numbers.

Syntax: MIN (number1, [number2, ... number_n])

Example:

	A	B	C	D	E	F	G
1	Value						
2	10.5		7.2				
3	7.2						
4	200						
5	5.4						
6	8.1						

C2 | f_x =MIN(A2, A3)

=MIN (A2, A3) Result is 7.2

MAX

The MAX function in MS Excel returns the highest value from a set of numbers.

Syntax: MAX (number1, [number2, ... number_n])

Example:

	A	B	C	D	E	F	G
1	Value						
2	10.5		10.5				
3	7.2						
4	200						
5	5.4						
6	8.1						

C2 | f_x =MAX(A2, A3)

=MAX (A2, A3) Result is 10.5

MEDIAN

The MEDIAN function in MS Excel returns the median of the numbers input.

Syntax: MEDIAN (number1, [number2, ... number_n])

Example:

=MEDIAN (A2, A3) Result is 8.85

MODE

The MODE function in MS Excel delivers the most commonly occurring number in a group of numbers.

Syntax: MODE (number1, [number2, ... number_n])

Example:

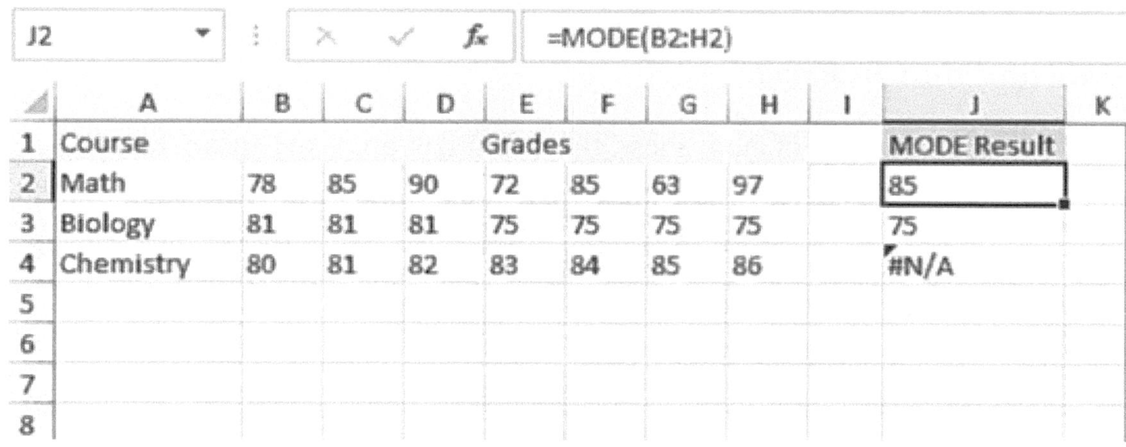

=MODE (B2:H2) Result is 85

MS Excel Date and Time

Incorporating the current time and date into an Excel spreadsheet may be advantageous for anyone who works as a financial analyst. This guide will explain how the current date and time function in Excel works, as well as demonstrate how it may be applied to your data analysis.

Excel formulas for calculating the current date and time (dynamic)

Two different formulas are available for use in your spreadsheet, depending on the type of information you wish to put in it.

Please keep in mind that these are dynamic formulas, which means they will update automatically every time a spreadsheet is opened.

Current date formula:

=TODAY()

Current time formula:

=NOW()

Current date and time in Excel

Examine a real-world example of how these two formulas are used in an Excel spreadsheet to demonstrate their functionality. The following screenshot demonstrates how each function operates as well as the output it produces. The following information will display in your spreadsheet if the formula is created on May 24, 2018, at 1:36 p.m., as an example.

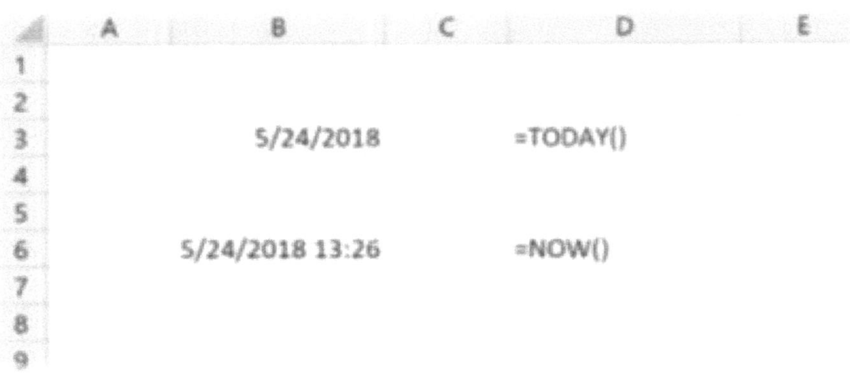

NOTE: When Excel displays the time, it does so using a 24-hour clock.

As you can see, the =TODAY() computation is just concerned with the current day, month, and year. When you use the =NOW() function to get more information, you'll get the current date as well as the month, year, hour, and minute (using a 24-hour clock).

Formulas for the current date and time in Excel (static)

You may not always wish for the figures in the file to be updated each time the file is opened. If this is the case, you should insert a static copy of the formulas.

Static formulas include the following:

"Ctrl +;" - this command inserts the date (Windows)

"Ctrl + Shift +;" – the date and time are inserted (Windows)

'COMMAND + (Mac)

Why would you want to include the current date and time in Excel?

Including the current date and time in an Excel worksheet might be helpful for various reasons. Assume you want users to be able to view the current time on the cover page of a financial model whenever they print it.

There are a variety of reasons why the time and date should be included:

- Creating a log of activity
- On a cover page
- When a document is printed
- For the purpose of version control
- When displaying time-sensitive data
- When cash flows are discounted to the present (Net Present Value and XNPV function)

How to format the date and time

You have the option of changing the date and time format that is used in the spreadsheet. To do so, use the F1 key on your keyboard (or right-click on the cell and click Format Cells). Click on Number and then on Date or Time to set the formatting for your spreadsheet once the Format Cells box appears on your screen.

MS Excel Financial Functions

If you are an investor and you do not know how to start using Financial Formulas in Microsoft Excel, you have come to the right place. There are many useful features in Excel for investors and savvy users alike. You can use the functions to calculate investment interest rates and yield to maturity of a security. You can also use these functions to determine the future value of money given a fixed interest rate and regular payments. For example, if you invested $25 million and received a 4.5% annual interest rate, you would receive a total return of $154.6 million over 30 years.

Financial Formulas in Microsoft Excel are built-in functions available in the spreadsheet. You can view a list of them on the Financial Functions page. The page has detailed information about each function and examples of its use. You can also see a list of all available financial functions by clicking on the Insert Function wizard and selecting the Financial category. Alternatively, you can type financial functions into the search bar or press F1.

Using Financial Formulas in Microsoft Excel is a great way to manage your finances. There are 53 different financial functions that can be used to calculate a number of things, from mortgage payments to car loan payments. Learn how to use these functions to organize your financial data for future use. There are also lots of other useful tools for Excel that you can use to keep track of your finances. So, go ahead and learn how to use Excel's financial functions to simplify your life and boost your business's bottom line.

Leveraging Excel's Financial functions

Excel has lots of financial functions. People use these functions to calculate their day-to-day activities in their company or firm. Some of the functions are Future Value (FV), FVSCHEDULE, Present Value (PV), XNPV, PPMT, and lots more. Below are some of the ways you can utilize these functions in Excel.

The FV function enables us to calculate the future value of an investment with a fixed interest rate.

The PMT function allows you to calculate the total payment—including principal and interest—paid per period of a fixed interest rate loan. This will help you to determine whether or not you can afford the repayments necessary to pay off the loan over a given period of time.

The structure necessary for the use of the PMT function is:

=PMT(rate, number_payments, present_value, future_value, type)

The rate is, as usual, the interest per period. The number_payments is self-explanatorily, it calculates how many payments the loan repayment would be split into.

The PV function calculates the present value of a loan or investment. When working with money over time, the value of that money fluctuates. This is not because of inflation, but because having money now is "better" than having the promise of money in the future. If you have money now, you can put it to good use, invest it, and so on. However, if you must wait to receive that money, you will be paying the "opportunity cost" of not having it right now, i.e. you would be unable to use or invest it.

This concept becomes very important when calculating the periodic values of assets and liabilities, such as those we have seen earlier in this chapter. In the following chapter, we will learn how to combine functions so as to use this PV function as part of a larger calculation. For now, let's take a look at the arguments included in the PV function itself.

=PV(rate, number_periods, period_payment, future_value, type)

As you can see, the PV function follows a familiar argument layout. Rate is the *periodic* interest rate, located first as usual. The number of periods is included as the second argument. The periodic payment is the fixed payment per period, as can be calculated using the PMT function above.

CONVERTING INTEREST RATES

Computing effective rate with FV

The Function Value (FV) is used to discover the future value of an investment. It contains an interest rate that doesn't change, and the payment is made periodically. To do this, the formula below is used;

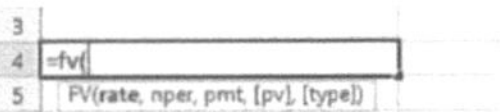

Rate here means the interest rate or the period. **Nper** means the number of periods.

[Pmt] means the payment period. **PV** means the Present Value. **[Type]** means when the payment is made. In this [type] option, when something is attached to it, it means that the payment was made at the period end.

Example: Apple invested $100 in 2017, and this payment has been made yearly. They have an interest of 10% per annum. What would be their future value in 2021?

	A	B
1		
2		
3	RATE	10%
4	NPER	3
5	PMT	1
6	PV	-100
7	TYPE	0
8		
9	=FV(B3,B4,B5,B6,B7)	
10	FV(rate, nper, **pmt**, [pv], [type])	

You will get the US $129.79

Creating an amortization schedule

This is done using the PMT function. We use it to compute the payment made monthly on a loan. It has an interest rate of 5%, a duration of two years, and a present value of $20000. Named ranges are used for the input cells.

=PMT(AnnualInterestRate/PaymentsPerYear,Years*PaymentsPerYear,Amount)

	A	B	C	D	E	F
1	Annual Interest Rate	5.00%				
2	Years	2				
3	Payments Per Year	12				
4	Amount	$20,000				
5						
6	Payment Number	Payment	Principal	Interest	Balance	
7	1	($877.43)				
8						

With the PPMT function, compute the principal part of the payment.

=PPMT(AnnualInterestRate/PaymentsPerYear,A7,Years*PaymentsPerYear,Amount)

	A	B	C	D	E	F
1	Annual Interest Rate	5.00%				
2	Years	2				
3	Payments Per Year	12				
4	Amount	$20,000				
5						
6	Payment Number	Payment	Principal	Interest	Balance	
7		1	($877.43)	($794.09)		
8						

Then, using the IPMT function, compute the payment with the interesting part.

=IPMT(AnnualInterestRate/PaymentsPerYear,A7,Years*PaymentsPerYear,Amount)

	A	B	C	D	E	F
1	Annual Interest Rate	5.00%				
2	Years	2				
3	Payments Per Year	12				
4	Amount	$20,000				
5						
6	Payment Number	Payment	Principal	Interest	Balance	
7		1	($877.43)	($794.09)	($83.33)	
8						

Fill in the balance.

=Amount+C7

	A	B	C	D	E	F
1	Annual Interest Rate	5.00%				
2	Years	2				
3	Payments Per Year	12				
4	Amount	$20,000				
5						
6	Payment Number	Payment	Principal	Interest	Balance	
7		1	($877.43)	($794.09)	($83.33)	$19,205.91	
8						

Pick range A7:E7. Then drag it down one row. Modify the balance formula.

```
=E7+C8
```

	A	B	C	D	E	F
1	Annual Interest Rate	5.00%				
2	Years	2				
3	Payments Per Year	12				
4	Amount	$20,000				
5						
6	Payment Number	Payment	Principal	Interest	Balance	
7	1	($877.43)	($794.09)	($83.33)	$19,205.91	
8	2	($877.43)	($797.40)	($80.02)	$18,408.50	
9						

Pick range A8:E8. Drag it down to row 30.

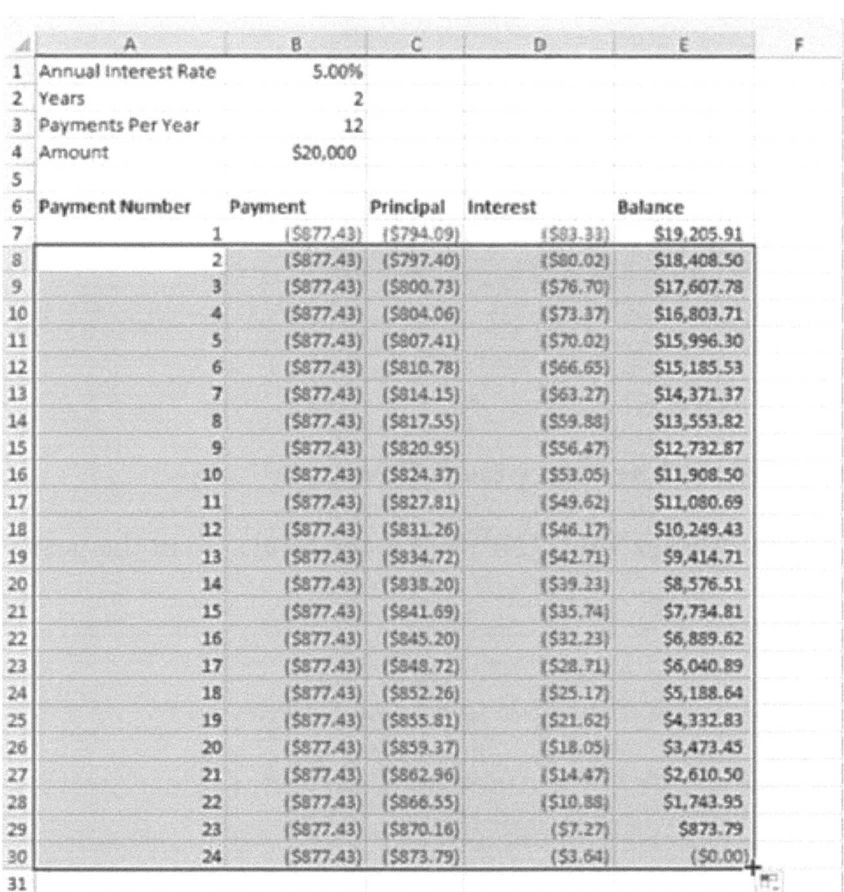

	A	B	C	D	E	F
1	Annual Interest Rate	5.00%				
2	Years	2				
3	Payments Per Year	12				
4	Amount	$20,000				
5						
6	Payment Number	Payment	Principal	Interest	Balance	
7	1	($877.43)	($794.09)	($83.33)	$19,205.91	
8	2	($877.43)	($797.40)	($80.02)	$18,408.50	
9	3	($877.43)	($800.73)	($76.70)	$17,607.78	
10	4	($877.43)	($804.06)	($73.37)	$16,803.71	
11	5	($877.43)	($807.41)	($70.02)	$15,996.30	
12	6	($877.43)	($810.78)	($66.65)	$15,185.53	
13	7	($877.43)	($814.15)	($63.27)	$14,371.37	
14	8	($877.43)	($817.55)	($59.88)	$13,553.82	
15	9	($877.43)	($820.95)	($56.47)	$12,732.87	
16	10	($877.43)	($824.37)	($53.05)	$11,908.50	
17	11	($877.43)	($827.81)	($49.62)	$11,080.69	
18	12	($877.43)	($831.26)	($46.17)	$10,249.43	
19	13	($877.43)	($834.72)	($42.71)	$9,414.71	
20	14	($877.43)	($838.20)	($39.23)	$8,576.51	
21	15	($877.43)	($841.69)	($35.74)	$7,734.81	
22	16	($877.43)	($845.20)	($32.23)	$6,889.62	
23	17	($877.43)	($848.72)	($28.71)	$6,040.89	
24	18	($877.43)	($852.26)	($25.17)	$5,188.64	
25	19	($877.43)	($855.81)	($21.62)	$4,332.83	
26	20	($877.43)	($859.37)	($18.05)	$3,473.45	
27	21	($877.43)	($862.96)	($14.47)	$2,610.50	
28	22	($877.43)	($866.55)	($10.88)	$1,743.95	
29	23	($877.43)	($870.16)	($7.27)	$873.79	
30	24	($877.43)	($873.79)	($3.64)	($0.00)	
31						

Calculating the net present value

This is done using the Present Value function. It is easier to calculate the present value if you can calculate the future value.

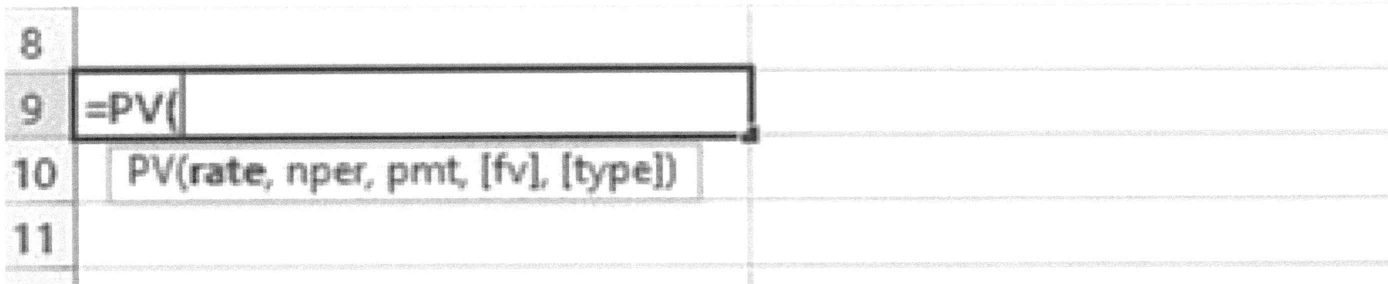

Example: The FV of investment in Canada was $100 in 2017. They make the payment yearly with an interest rate of 10% per annum. Calculate the present value?

◢	A	B	C	D
1				
2				
3	RATE	10%		
4	NPER	3		
5	PMT	1		
6	FV	-100		
7	TYPE	0		
8				
9	=PV(B3,B4,B5,B6,B7			
10	PV(rate, nper, pmt, [fv], [type])			
11				

You will have $72.64

Calculating the positive and negative cash flows

This is done using the Net Present Value (NPV). It is the total sum of the positive and negative cash flows over the years.

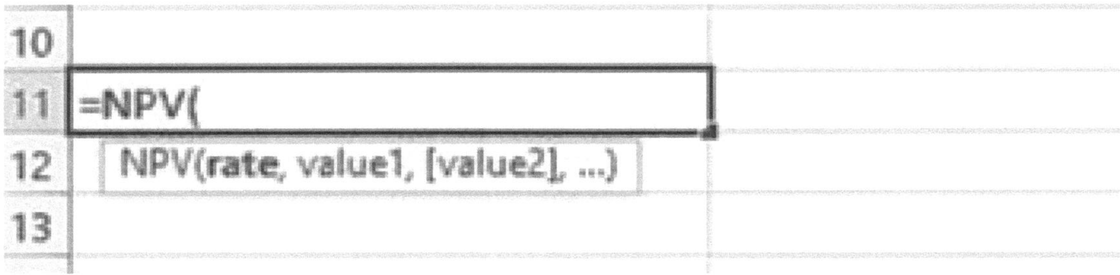

Rate means the discount rate for some time. The Values mean the positive or negative cash flows. Negative values are seen as payments, while positive values are seen as inflows.

Example: You will get $240.87.

	A	B	C	D	E
1					
2		Details	In US $		
3		Rate of Discount	5%		
4		Initial Investment	-1000		
5		Return from 1st year	300		
6		Return from 2nd year	400		
7		Return from 3rd year	400		
8		Return from 4th year	300		
9					
10		=NPV(C3,C5:C8)+C4			
11					

Statistical Functions

Statistical Functions in MS Excel help you perform basic and more complex calculations. Linear regression is one of the statistical functions used to predict future values based on current values. MAX and MIN functions are also useful to find the maximum and minimum value of a data set. CLEAN function removes nonprintable characters from text and is useful when importing text. It also performs calculations on imported data. Let's have a look at how they work.

Rounding off numbers

When using the ROUND function in MS Excel, you can either round off or up the number. The ROUNDUP function rounds numbers away from zero. For example, in cell B5, the ROUNDUP function will round pi to 3.14. The ROUNDDOWN function rounds numbers toward zero. Using the rounded-off value in cell B3 instead of the original value gives the result as 3.

ROUND

The ROUND function in MS Excel returns a number that has been rounded to a given number of digits. The ROUND function is an Excel built-in function that is classified as a Math Function.

Example:

		C1			f_x	=ROUND(A1, 0)	
	A	B	C	D	E	F	G
1	662.79		663				
2	54.1						
3							
4							
5							
6							

=ROUND (A1, 0) 663

ROUNDOWN

Produces a number that has been rounded down to a specified number of digits.

Syntax: ROUNDDOWN (number, digits)

For example:

C1			f_x =ROUNDDOWN(A1, 0)			
	A	B	C	D	E	F	G
1	662.79		662			
2	54.1					
3						
4						
5						
6						

ROUNDUP

Produces a number that has been rounded up to a specified number of digits.

Syntax: ROUNDUP (number, digits)

Example:

C1			f_x =ROUNDUP(A1, 0)			
	A	B	C	D	E	F	G
1	662.79		663			
2	54.1					
3						
4						
5						
6						

POWER and SQTR

The POWER and SQTR statistical functions in Microsoft Excel let you calculate various statistics with the help of formulas. The SQRT function returns the square root of cell B3 and is used to calculate the square root of a number. However, the SQTR function is only used for focused purposes. It returns a result of two when used with a range of numbers. The POWER function, on the other hand, allows you to calculate the exponent of any number, which means the power to which you want to raise a base value.

This function calculates the correlation between two variables, and also the difference between two values. It is also used to calculate the effect of a variable on a group of data. It is a great tool for performing statistical analysis on a variety of data. To use this function, just enter the values into the formula and click the calculate button.

POWER

The POWER function is an Excel built-in function that is categorized as a Math Function. It returns the result of raising a number to a specific power.

Example:

C1			f_x	=POWER(A1, A2)			
	A	B	C	D	E	F	G
1	3		81				
2	4						
3	4.5						
4							
5							
6							

The following POWER samples would be returned based on the Excel file above:

The result of =POWER (A1, A2) is 81.

SQRT

The SQRT function is an Excel built-in function that is classified as a Number Function. This Excel function calculates the square root of an integer.

Syntax: SQRT (number)

Example:

	A	B	C	D	E	F	G
C1			=SQRT(A1)				
1	25		5				
2	33.6						
3	-5.2						
4							
5							
6							

=SQRT (A1)

Result is 5

SUM of the parts

If you have a range of data, you can use a statistical function to determine each part's average value. A statistical function is a more advanced method for calculating averages. These functions operate on numeric data, while formulas work on qualitative data. For example, the AVERAGE function will return the arithmetic mean of a cell range. Another common statistical function is the MODE function. The latter works similarly to the former, but is more useful for analysts.

There are a variety of statistical functions in Excel. The SUM function is one such example. It adds the values in multiple cells. To use this function, simply highlight the cells that have values you wish to sum. This function is especially useful for creating a Personal Budget. In addition to the SUM function, you can also use the COUNT and MAX functions to determine the highest and lowest values in a range.

Conditional summing

You can calculate the total of a series of values based on specified criteria. To use conditional summing in MS Excel, you must first specify the criteria. You can use the DMAX and DMIN statistical functions to find the highest and lowest value. This way, you can use conditional statistics to compare two sets of data. As long as the criteria are correct, you can perform calculations with conditional summing.

If you want to add values in a range, you can use the =SUMIF function. The function adds values in cells that meet the conditions. Here's an example: to see the production values of a company with three shifts, you'll use the criteria to determine which cells to add. This way, you can determine the value that best matches the criteria. If you want the sum to be case-sensitive, you need to use the SUMPRODUCT function with EXACT.

Chart and Graphics

Companies of all sizes and across a variety of industries use Excel to store data. Excel can help you transform spreadsheet data into charts and graphs so you can see your data clearly and make informed business decisions.

1.57 What are Excel Charts

A chart is a visual representation of data that is organized in rows and columns. Charts are often used to evaluate large data sets to identify trends and patterns.

Suppose you've been tracking sales data in Excel for the past three years. With charts, it's simple to figure out which year had the highest sales. You can also make charts to show how well you met your goals and did well.

1.58 Types of Charts

There are many different chart types in Microsoft Excel:

- Column Charts.

- Pie Charts

- Bar Charts.

- Line Charts.

- Combo Charts.

- Scatter Charts.

Column Charts

It is common for a Column Chart to show the categories on the horizontal (type) axis and the values on the vertical (value) axis simultaneously. To create a column chart, add data in columns or rows. You can use this tool when you want to compare values in your data set. The values are ordered vertically.

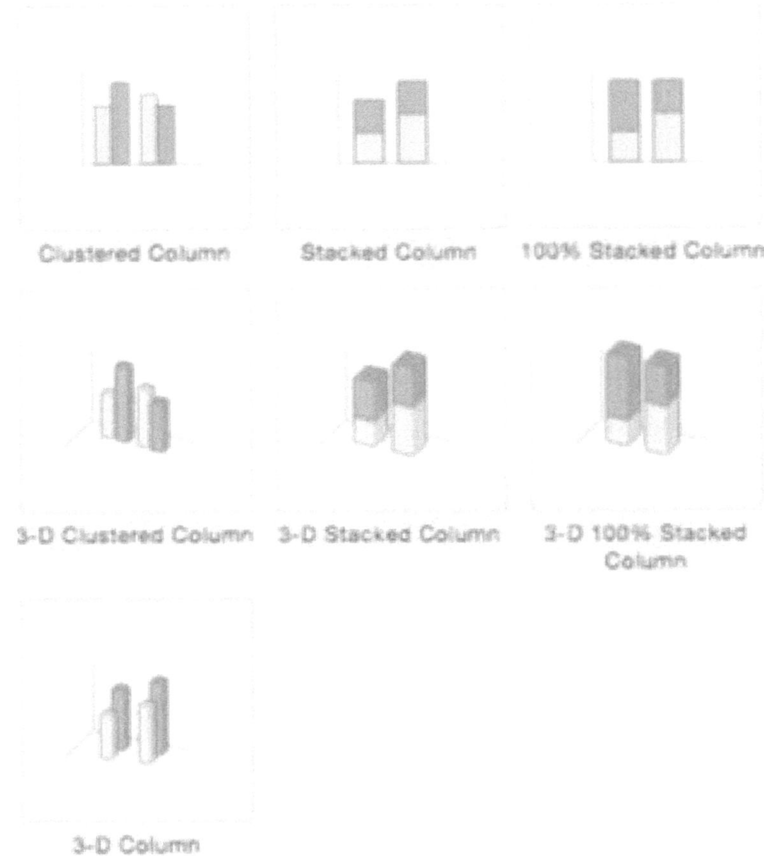

Pie Charts

We can plot a pie chart to represent data arranged in a column or row in a spreadsheet. Pie charts display element size for a data series in proportion to the total of the elements. The data points are shown as a percentage or portion of the whole pie chart.

This chart is recommended when:

- Only a single data series exists.

- None of your data values are negative.

- Nearly none of your data values are zeros.

- You have less than seven groupings, all of them representing parts of the complete pie chart.

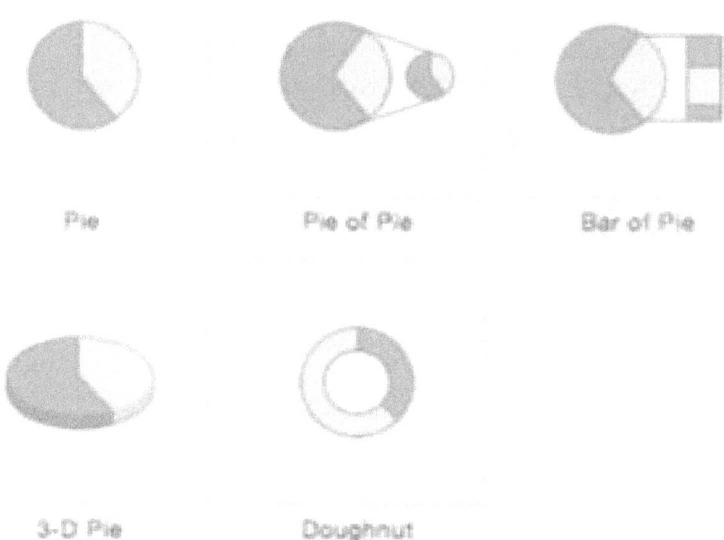

Bar Charts

The most significant distinction between a bar chart and a column chart is that the bars in a bar chart are horizontal rather than vertical in orientation. Although both bar charts and column charts are often used, some people prefer column charts when dealing with negative numbers since negatives are easier to discern when shown vertically on a y-axis.

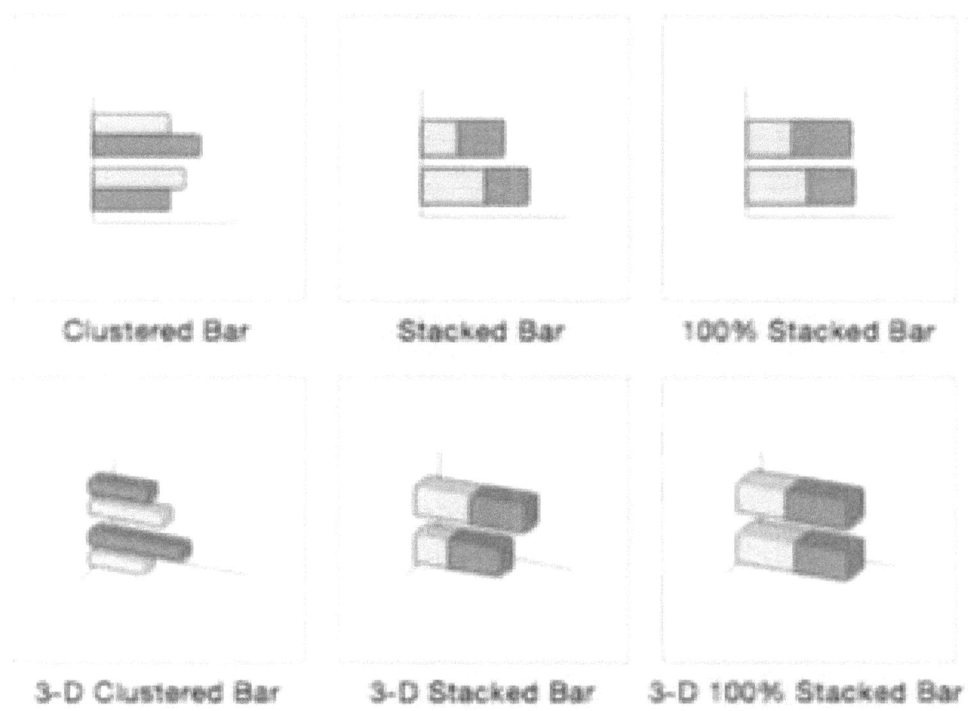

Line Charts

Line charts can display data that varies over time on a uniformly sized axis. They are perfect for this type of representation since they show data patterns at regular intervals, such as months, quarters, or years. You can use line charts to show how things have changed over time, like months, days, or years.

Combo Charts

The data is easier to understand when two or more chart types are used together, especially when the data is very different. It's shown with a second axis, making it even easier to see and read. A Combo chart can be made by first putting the data in columns and rows on a spreadsheet. You can use it when you want to show off different types of information at the same time.

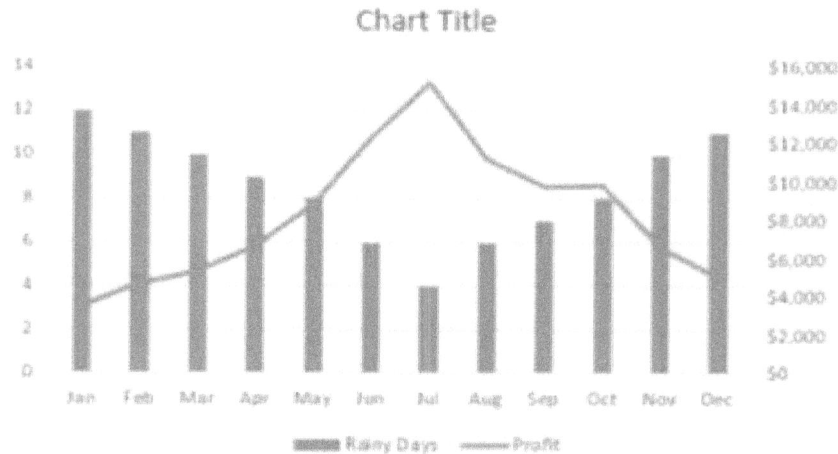

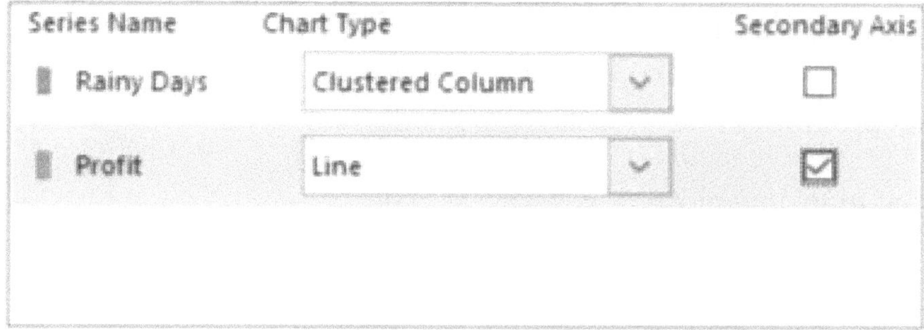

Bubble Charts

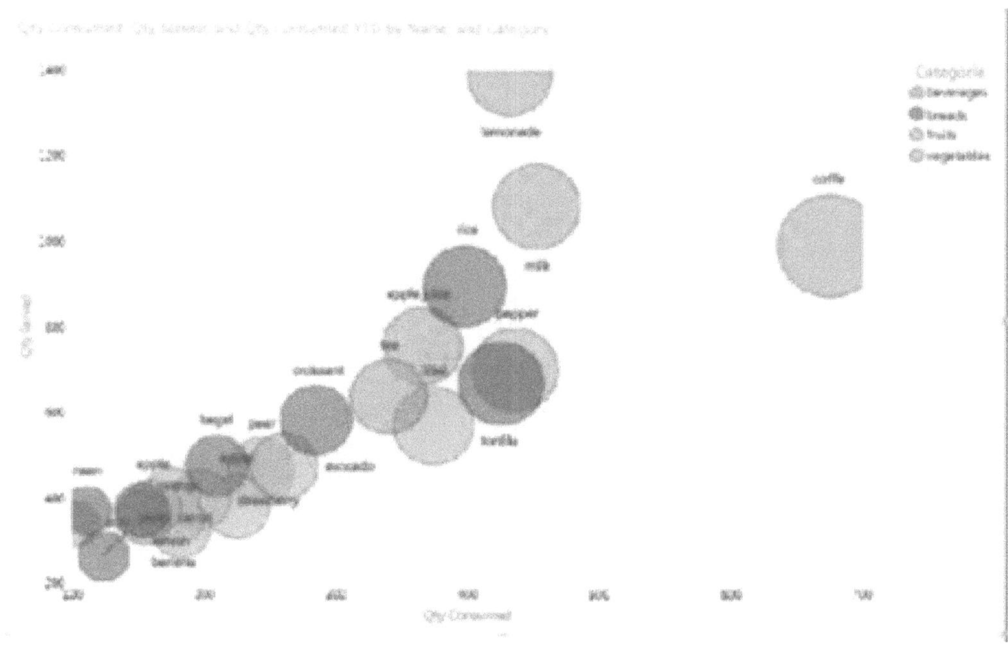

A Bubble graph appears similar to a Scatter graph but with an additional third column to clarify the scale of the bubbles that depict data points therein data sequence.

The subtypes of the Bubble Chart are as follows:

- Bubbles

- A three-dimensional visual effect bubble

- Stock Chart

Stock style charts, as the name implies, will show price changes in stocks. Nonetheless, the Stocks Chart can be used to show changes in other figures, such as average rainfall or annual temperatures.

Place data into rows or columns in a specific order onto a worksheet to make a Stock graph. The subtypes of the Stocks Chart are as follows:

- High-low-proximity

- Amount of high-low-close

- Volume of Open-High-Close

- Open- closer-Higher-Lower

Scatter Charts

Scatter charts are used to display how one variable influences another. They are similar to line graphs in that they help display changes in variables over time. (This is referred to as correlation.) Bubble charts, which are a common chart type, are classified as scatter.

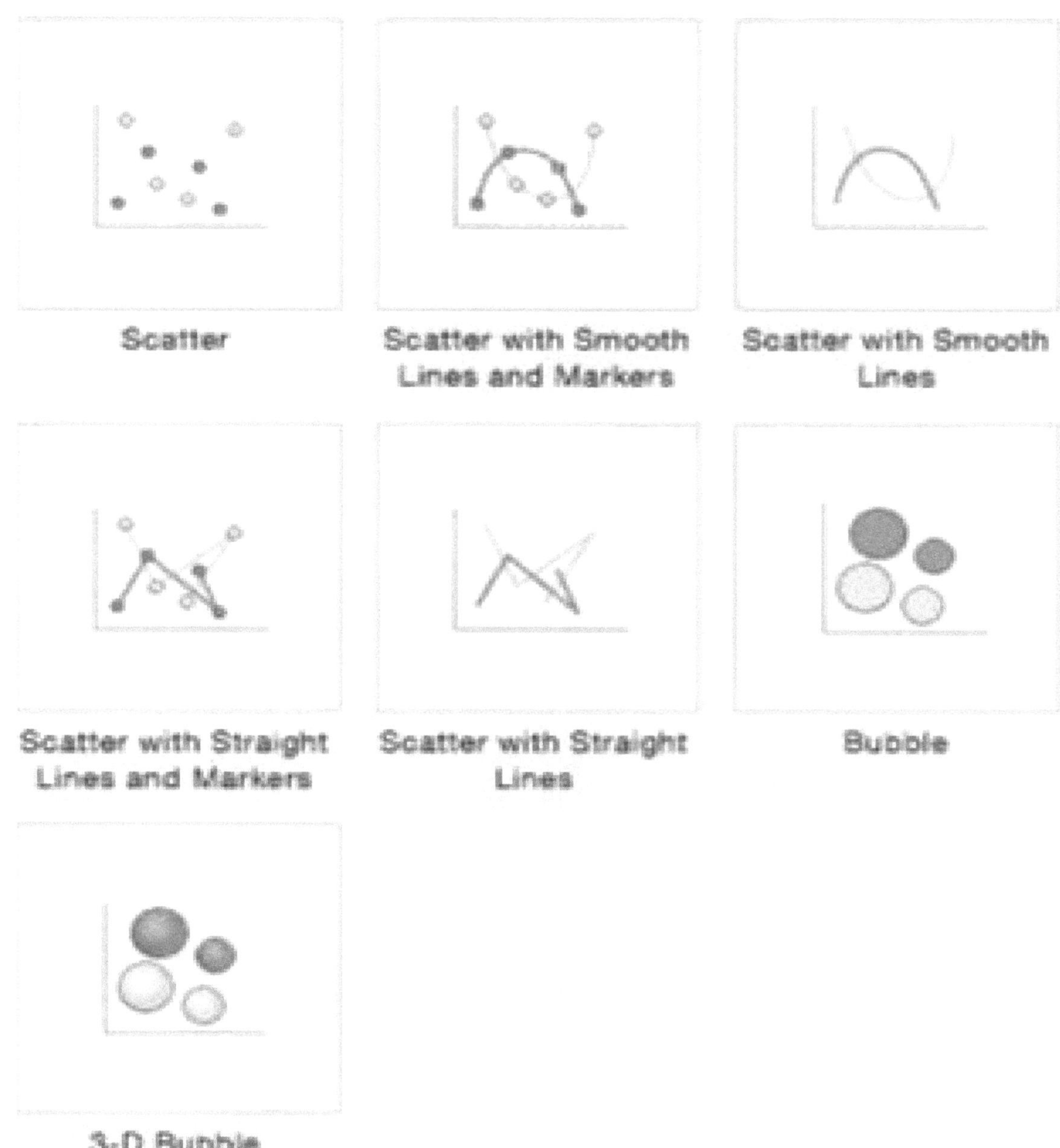

These are the seven scatter chart choices.

There are additional four charts categories. These charts are more case-specific:

- Area Charts.

- Stock Charts.

- Surface Charts.

- Radar Charts.

Area Charts

Area charts, like line charts, are used to illustrate how values change over time. Region charts on the other hand are good for highlighting variances in change across a number of variables since the area beneath each line is solid.

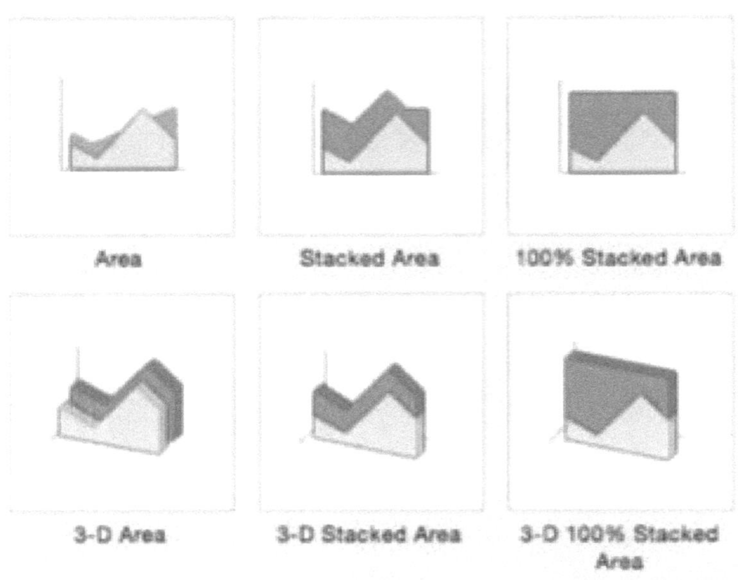

Stock Charts

Investors use this form of chart to show the low, high, and closing price of a stock and financial analysis. However, if you choose to represent the range of a value (or the range of its expected value) and its exact value, you can use them in every case.

Surface Charts

To represent data over a 3-D landscape, use a surface chart. Big data sets, data sets of more than two variables, and data sets with groups inside a single variable benefit from the additional plane. Surface charts can be difficult to understand, so make sure the audience is comfortable with them.

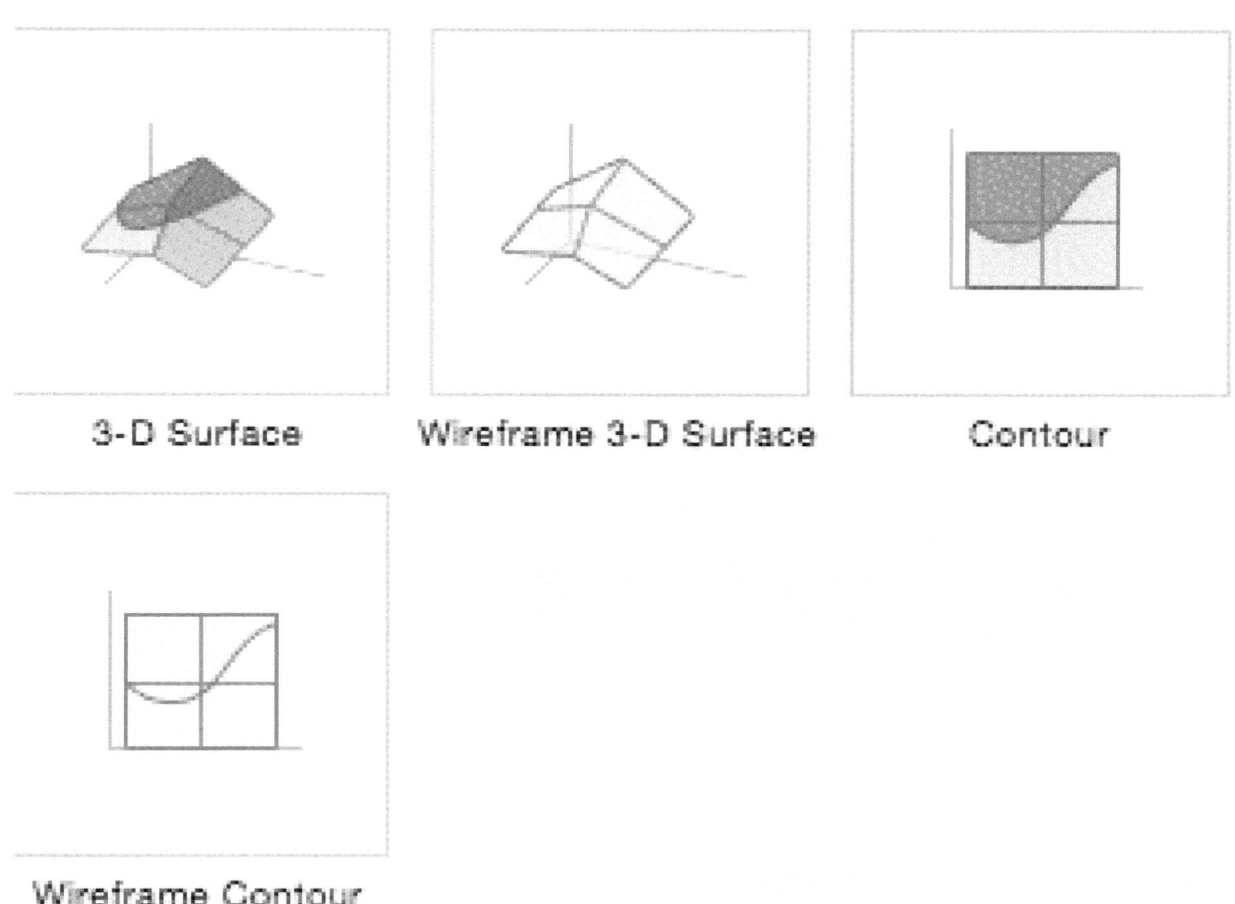

These are its types.

Radar Charts

A radar chart is useful for displaying data from different variables in relation to one another. The central point is the starting point for all variables. The trick to using radar charts is to compare all particular factors in relation to one another; they are often used to compare the weaknesses and strengths of various products or employees.

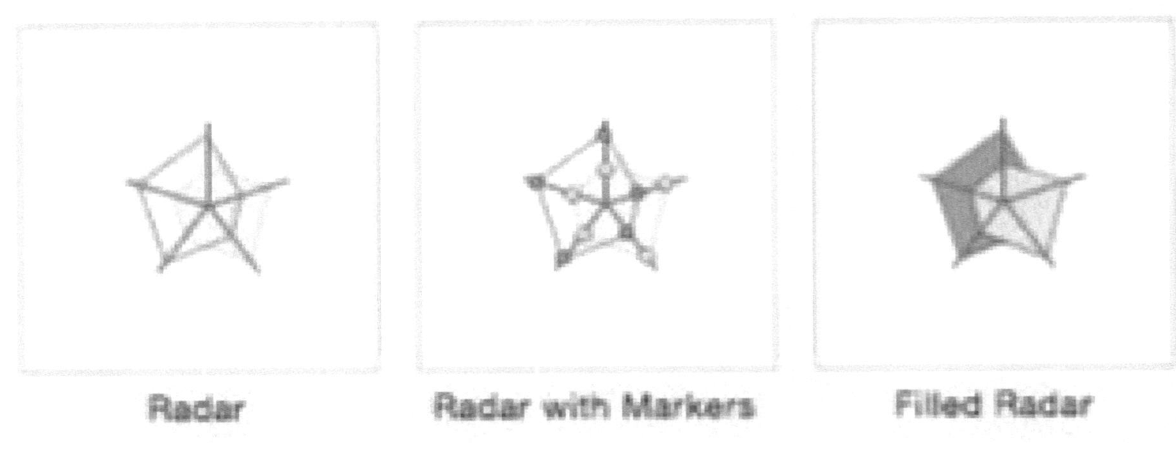

These are the three kinds of radar charts.

Use of Different Excel Charts

Different Charts Have a Variety of Applications

Here are some examples of how you can use different Excel charts:

1. Column Chart:

You can compare data from similar categories and see how the independence of variables changes over time using column charts. Compare and contrast the contributions of various class members and the differences in negative and positive values.

2. Bar Chart:

When the axis labels are too long to fit in a column chart, you may want to consider using a bar chart.

3. Pie Chart:

When you want to present a data composition that is 100 percent accurate, a pie chart is the best choice. In other words, a pie chart should only be used to represent the data when there is just one set of data and less than five categories to display on the chart. In general, pie charts represent your data's relationship between parts and the whole. When your data is given as a percentage, a pie chart is the most appropriate visual representation of the information. A pie chart should only be used when displaying data composition if the pie portions are of the same size.

4. Scatter Chart:

A scatter chart is a good option to consider when assessing and presenting the connection between two variables.

5. Line chart:

Line charts are used to display and draw attention to data patterns, especially long-term trends between data values. Another situation in which a line chart may be appropriate is when you have a large number of data points to present, and a column or bar chart would be too cluttered.

1.59 Charting Worksheet Data

1.59.1 Customizing and Formatting Elements of a chart

You can improve a graph or chart by adding chart components that explain features or add meaning to the whole illustration. Using the Add Chart Feature drop-down menu in the top-left corner, you can choose a chart element (below the Home tab).

To Hide or Display Axes

- Axes can be selected. Excel automatically pulls the column and row headers from your selected cell set to display horizontal and vertical axes on your chart (Under Axes, there is a checkmark beside Primary Horizontal and Primary Vertical.)

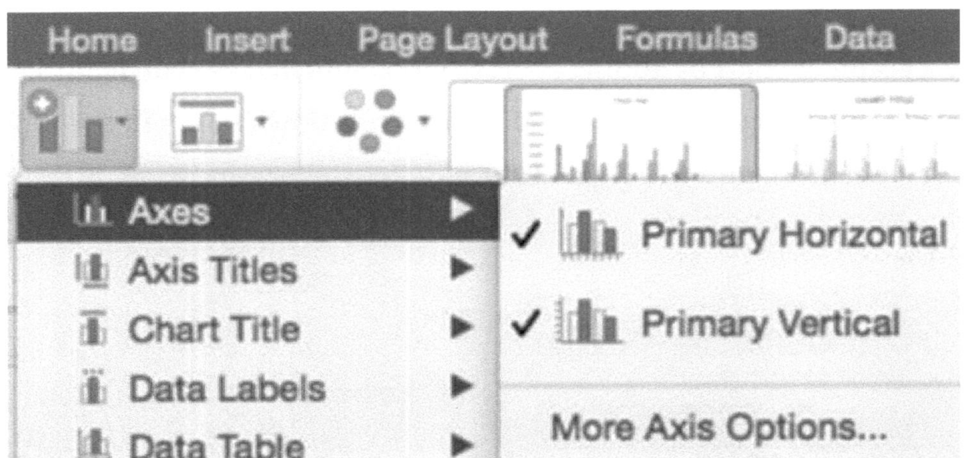

- To delete the view axis from the chart, uncheck these choices. In this case, selecting Primary Horizontal deletes the year labels from your chart's horizontal axis.

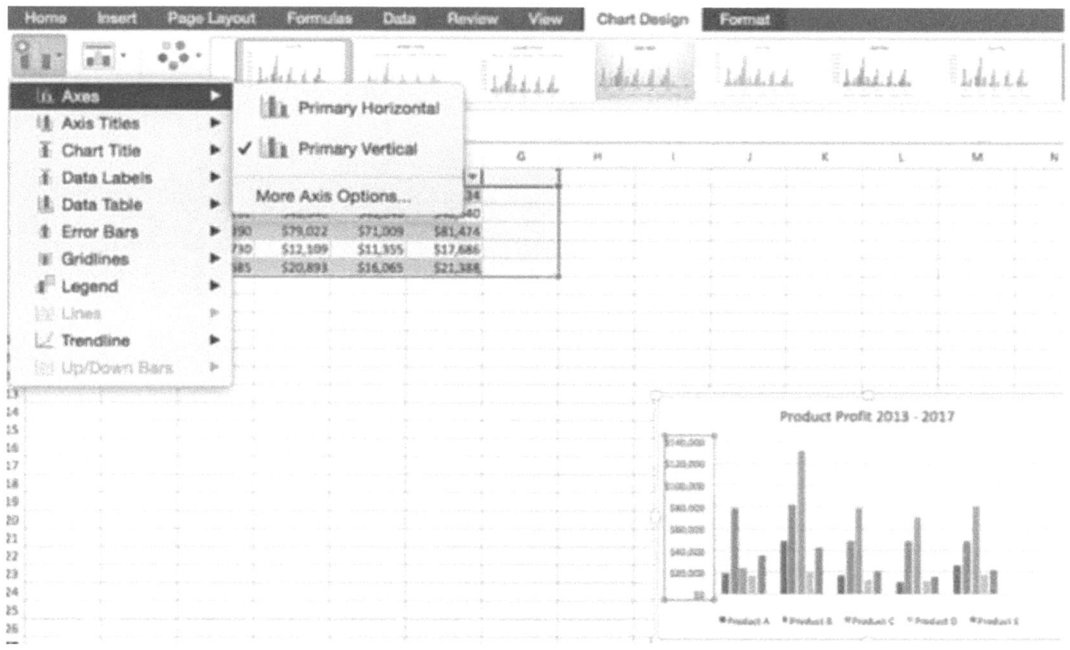

More Axis Choices... opens a window with extra formatting and text options, such as inserting tick marks, identifiers, or numbers, or the changing text color and height, from the Axes drop-down menu.

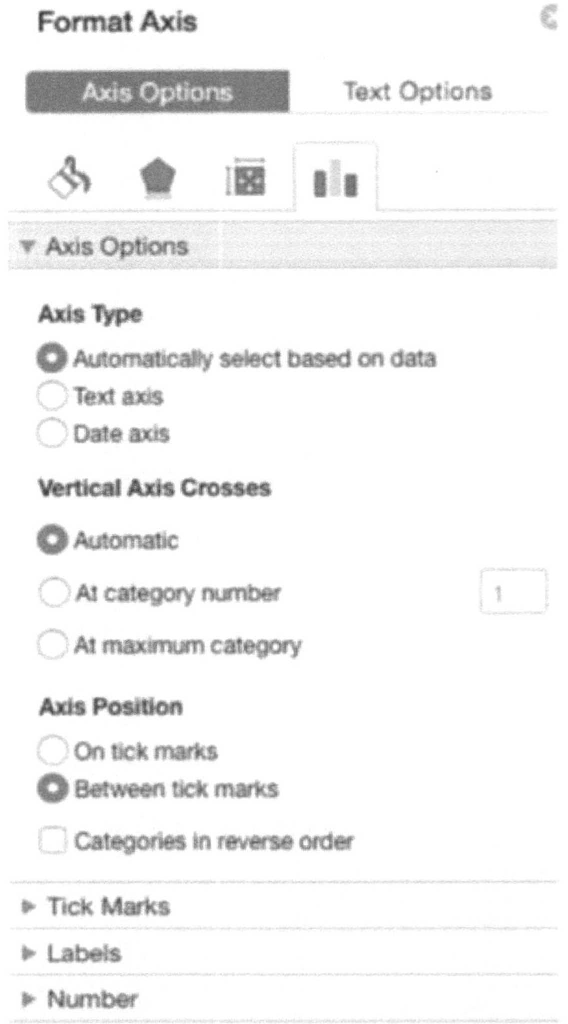

To Add Axis Titles

Select Axis Title from the drop-down menu after clicking Add the Chart Element. Since axis names are not immediately added to charts in Excel, either the Primary Horizontal or Primary Vertical will be uncontrolled.

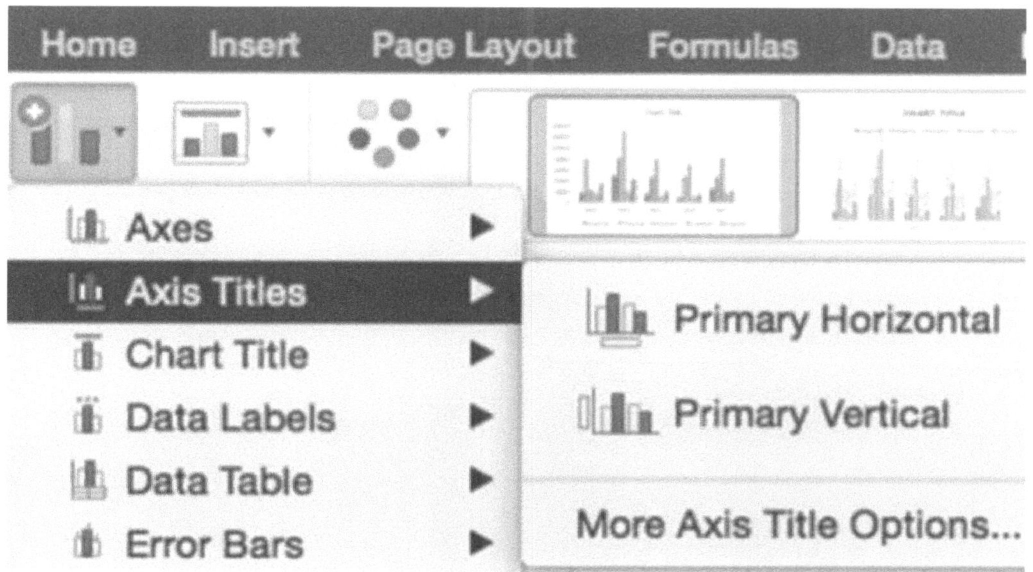

A script box will appear here on the chart when you press Primary Horizontal and Primary Vertical to generate axis names. In this case, press both. Fill in the axis titles. Add the titles "Year" and "Profit" to this example.

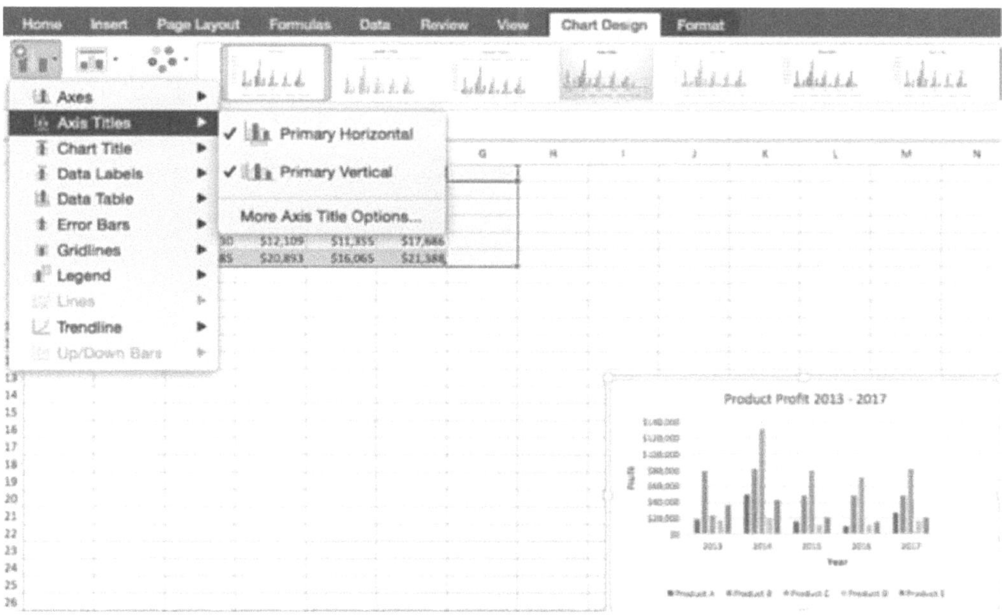

To Move or Remove Chart Title

Select Chart Title from the Add Chart Elements in the drop-down menu. The four options available are None, Above the Chart, Focused Overlay, and Further Title Choices.

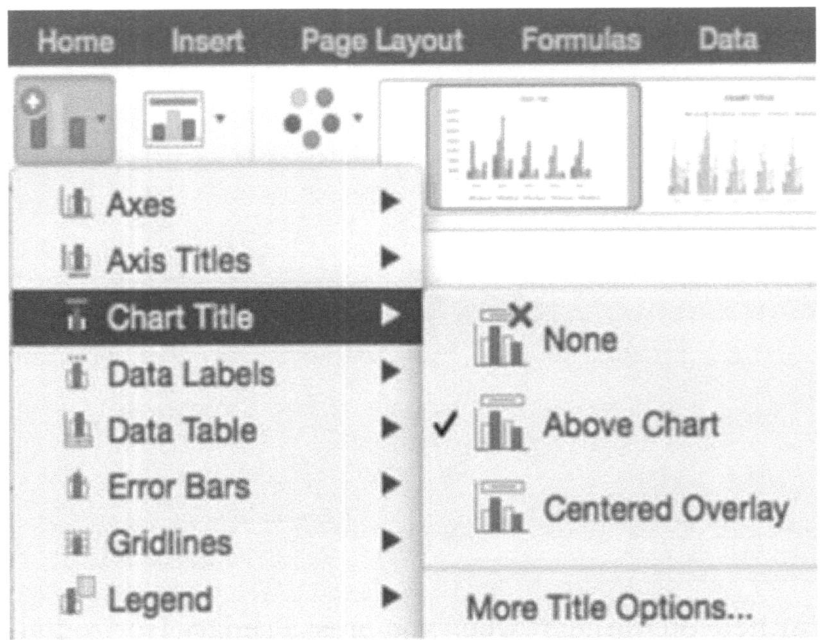

To delete the chart title, choose None.

To put a title above your chart, click Above Chart. Excel will automatically put a chart title above your chart if you make one.

To put the title inside the chart's gridlines, choose Centered Overlay. This alternative should be used with caution: you wouldn't want your title to obscure any of the data or clutter the graph (like in this example below).

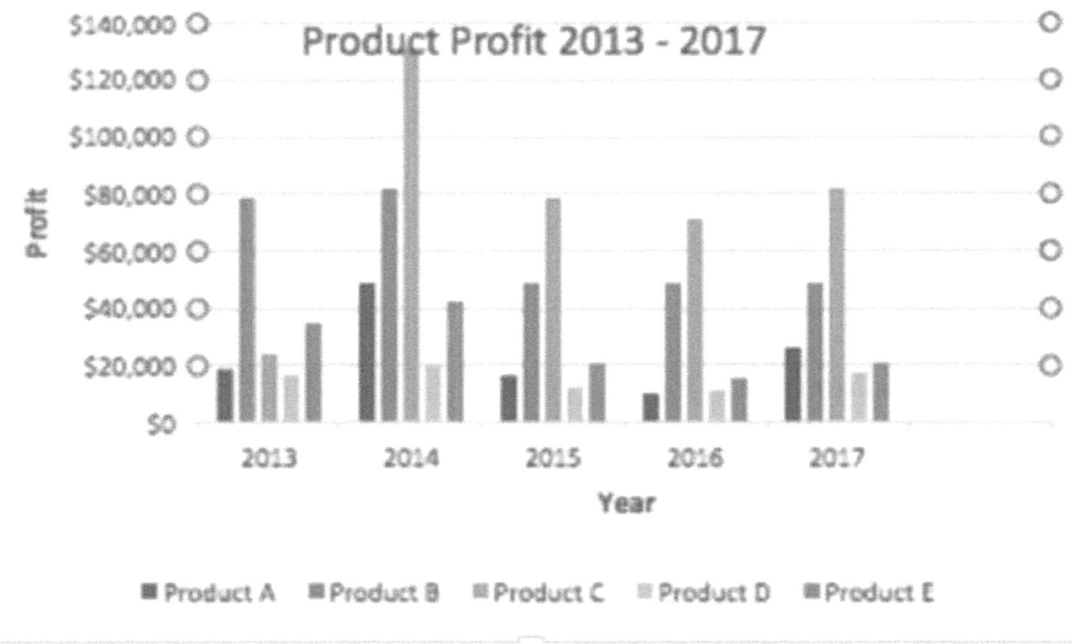

To Add Data Labels

Select Data Labels from the Add Chart Elements menu. For the data labels titles, there are six options: Middle, Inside End, Outside End, Inside Base, and More.

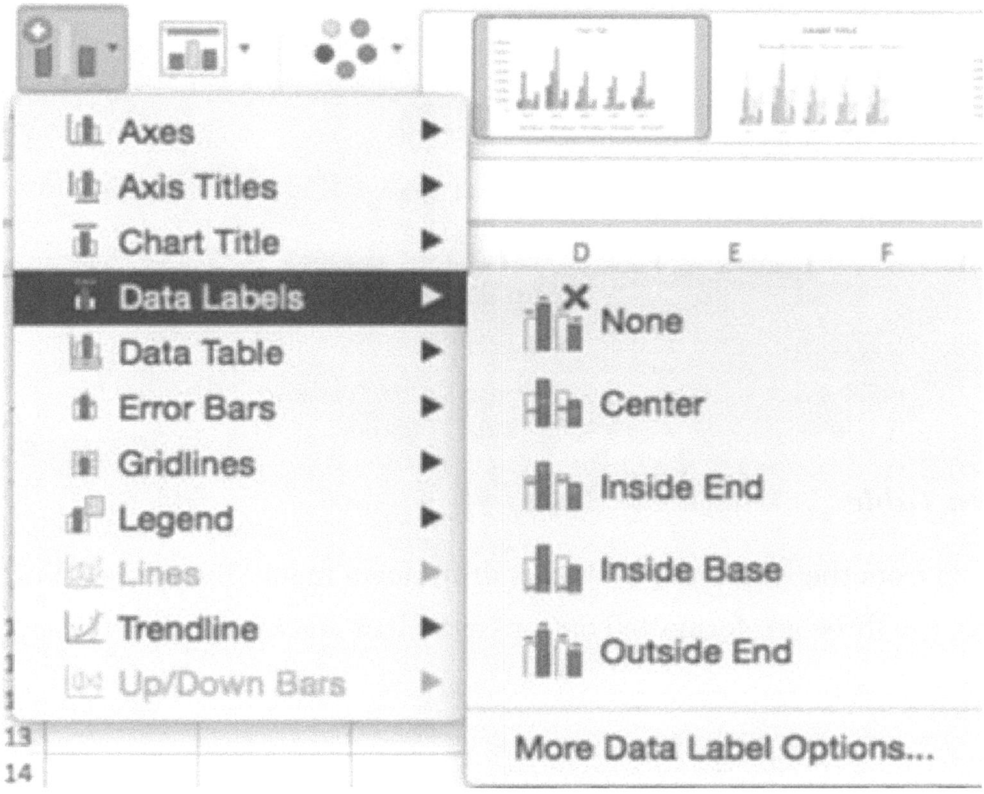

Every data point calculated in your map has a unique mark thanks to the four positioning choices. Select the desired option. If you have a limited number of detailed data points or a lot of extra room in the chart, this customization may be useful. Adding data labels to the chart (clustered column), on the other hand, would certainly appear cluttered. This is how choosing the Center data label would appear, for instance.

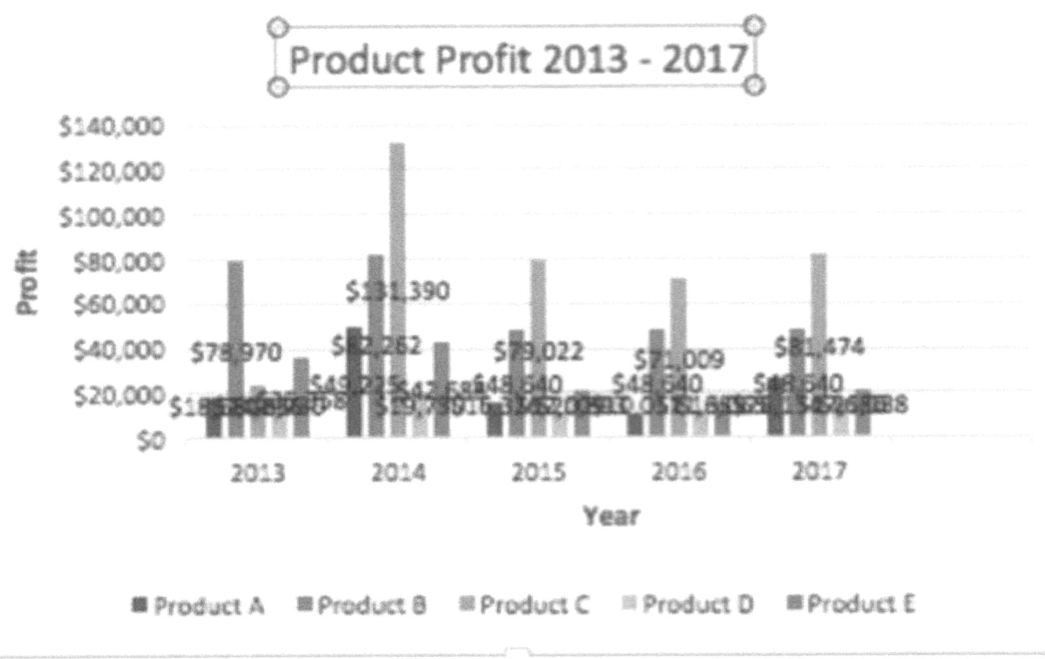

To Add a Data Table

Select Data Table from the Add Chart Elements drop-down menu. By pressing Further Data Table Choices, you can use three pre-formatted options as well as an expanded menu:

1. The default setting is None, which means that a data table isn't duplicated inside a chart.

2. Legend Keys shows the data set by displaying a data table under the list. The legend is color-coded as well.

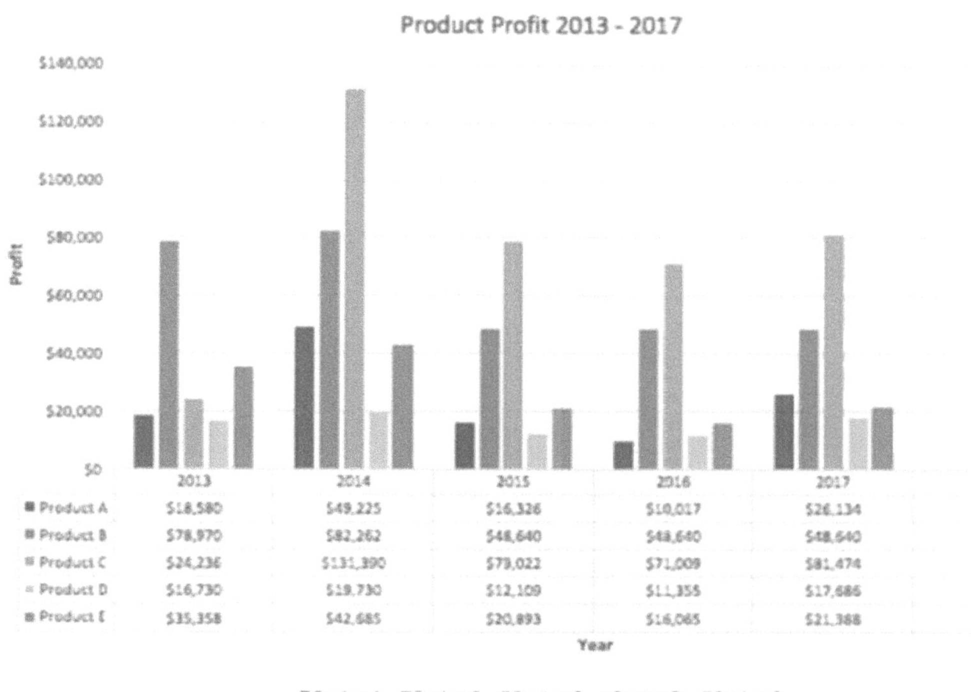

3. A data table is often shown underneath the chart with No Legend Keys but without a legend.

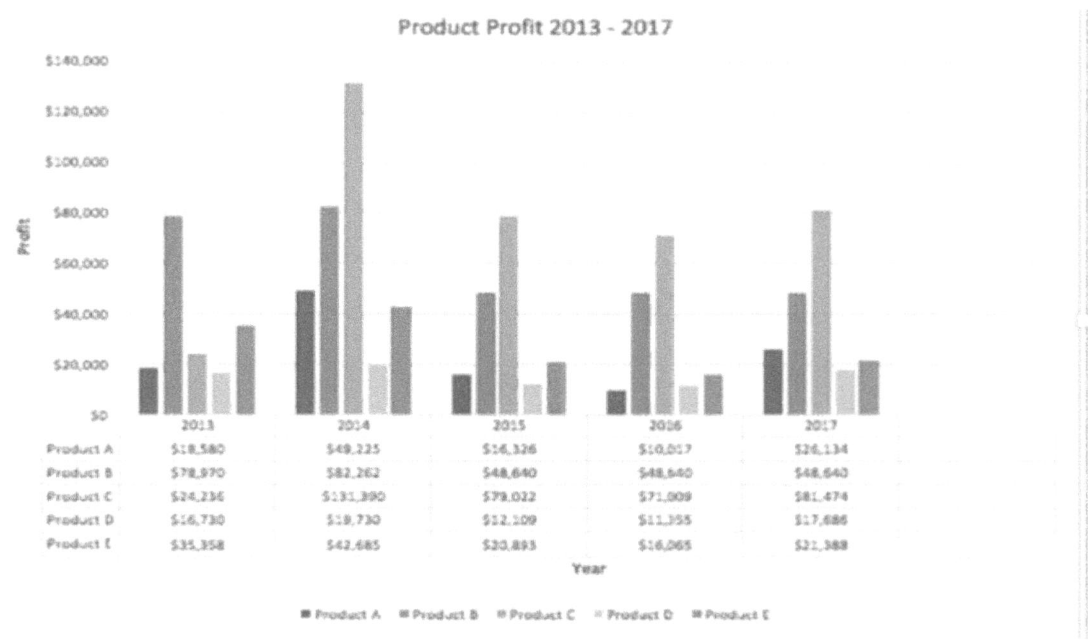

Note: If you plan to add a data table, you'll need to expand your chart to make room for it. Click on the corner and move it to the desired height to scale your chart.

To Add Error Bars

Select Error Bars from the Add Chart Elements menu. There are four choices on More Error Bar Options: None (default), 5% (Percentage), Standard Error, and Standard Deviation. Error bars offer a visual image of a possible error in the displayed results using various standard equations to isolate errors.

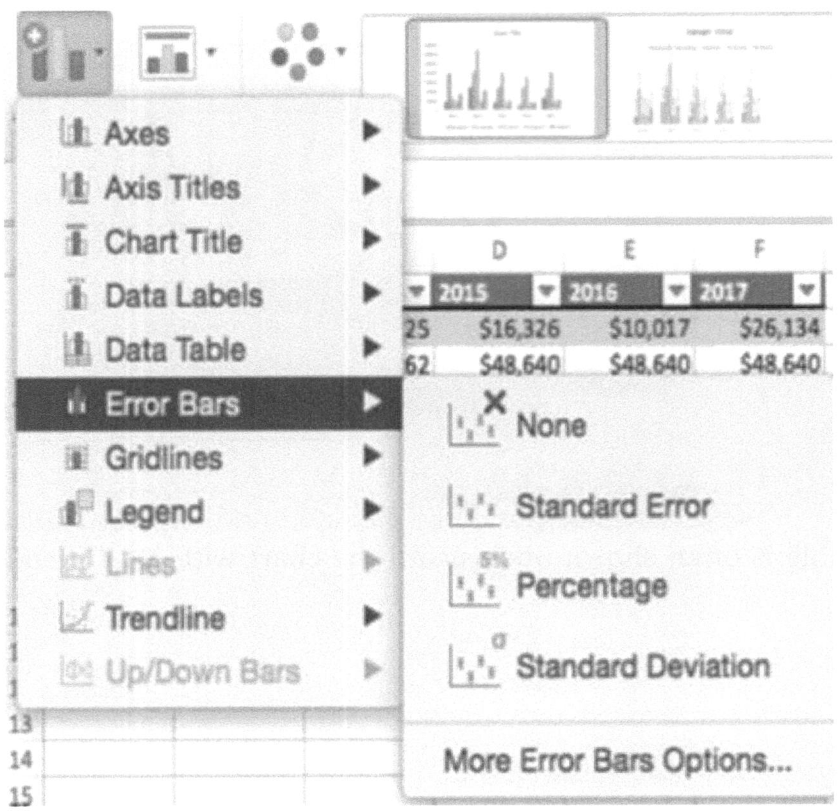

When you choose Standard Error from the choices, you will see a chart like the one shown below.

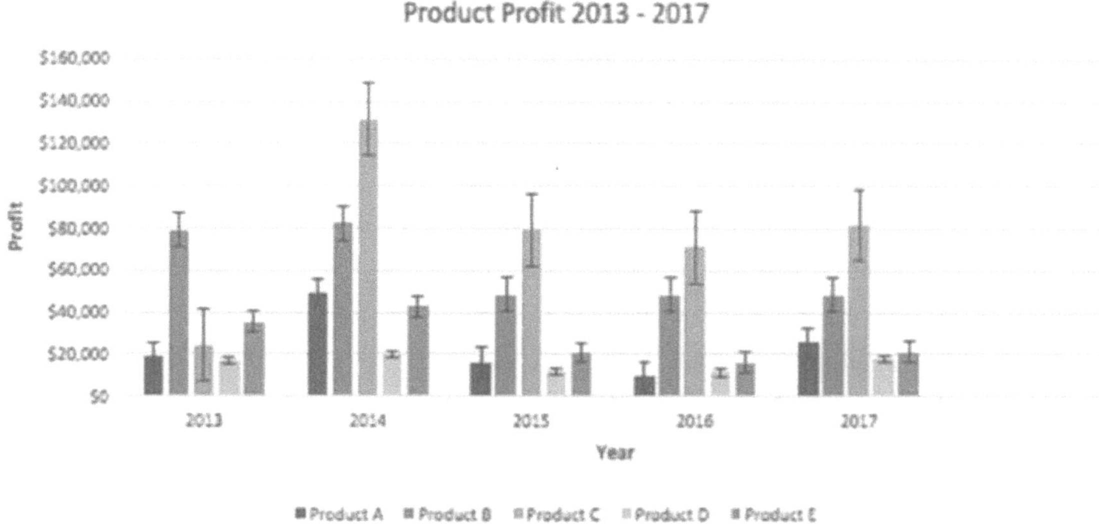

To Add Gridlines

Gridlines can be added to a chart by clicking Add Chart Elements and then Gridlines. There are four variations: Prime Major Horizontal, Prime Major Vertical, Prime Minor Horizontal, and Prime Minor Vertical. Although there are many Gridlines Options, Excel automatically adds Prime Major Horizontal gridlines to a column table.

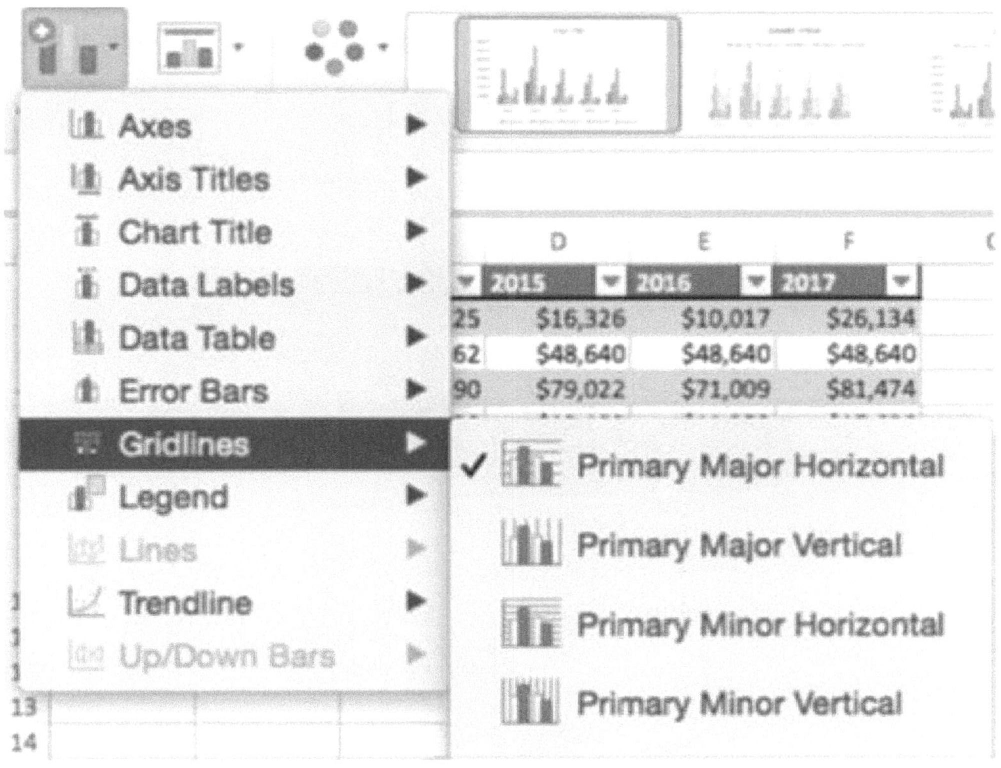

By pressing all the options, you can add as many distinct gridlines as you want. Here's how your chart would appear with all four gridline choices selected:

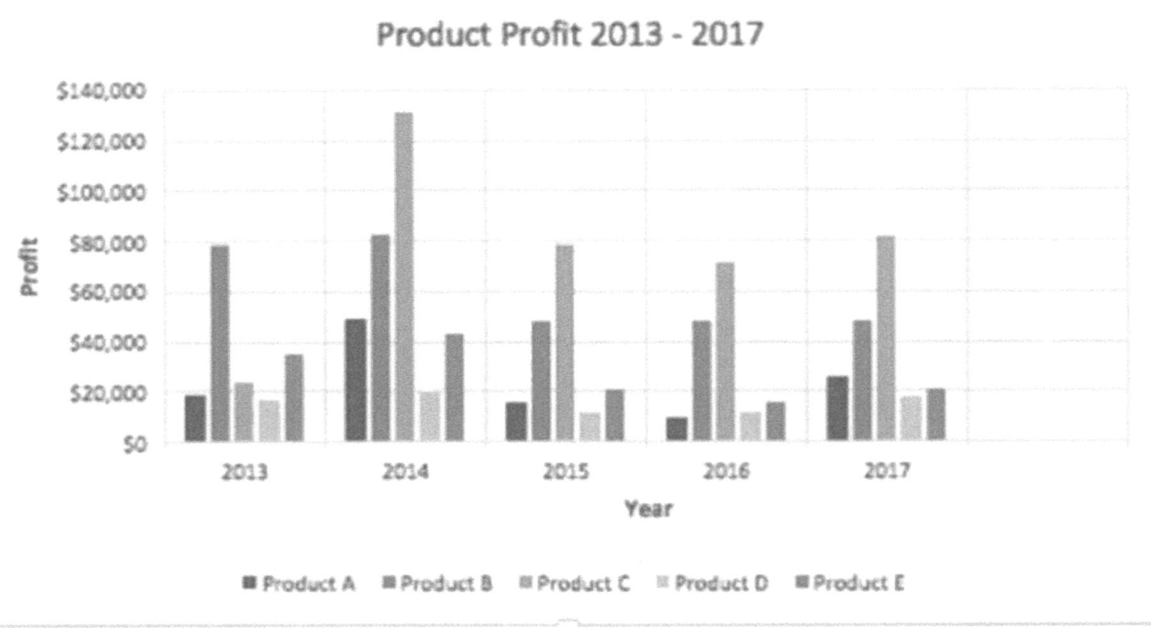

To Add a Legend

Select Legend from the Add Chart Elements drop-down menu. There are five legend positioning options in contrast to the many Legend Preferences: None, Correct, Top, Left, and Bottom.

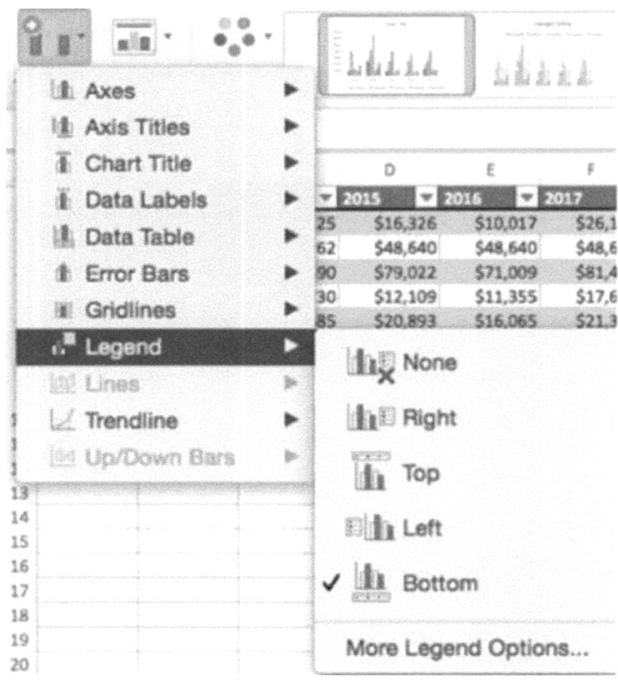

The type and format of the chart will determine where the legend is placed. Select the option that appears to be the most appealing on your graph. When you choose the placement of the Right legend, this is what your chart looks like:

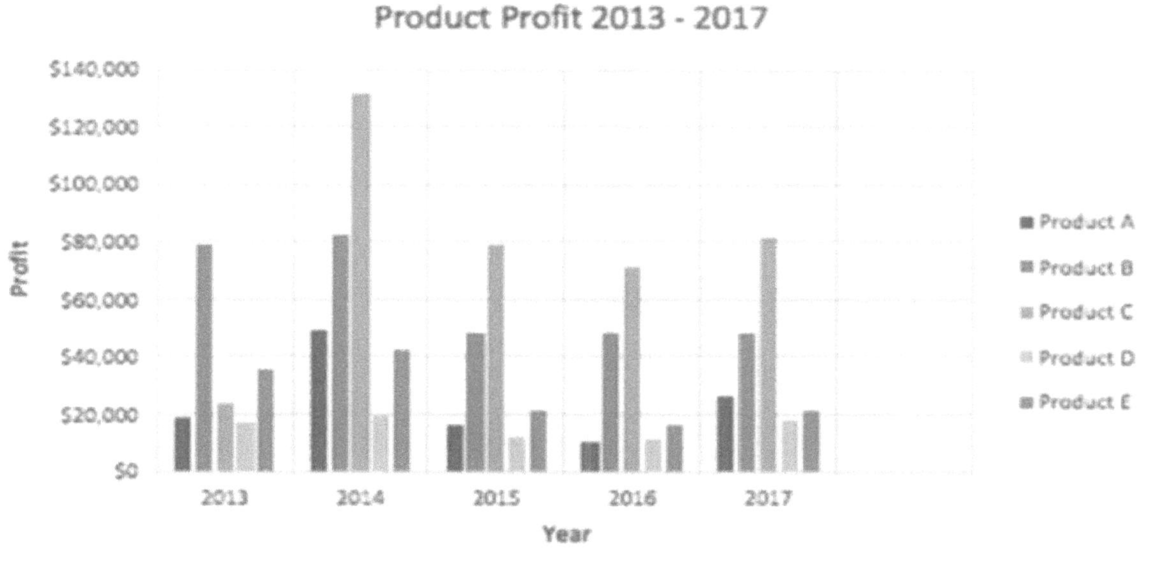

Adding Lines to a Clustered Column Chart: Lines aren't accessible for column charts (clustered). However, in some chart categories where you are comparing two factors, you can add lines to the chart after making the right choice (e.g., goal, average, comparison, etc.).

To Add a Trendline

Select Trendline from the Add Chart Elements drop-down menu. There are five choices: None (default), Linear Forecast, Linear, Exponential, and Moving Average, compared to Further Trendline Options. Be sure you're using the right tool for the data collection. In this case, you'll choose Linear.

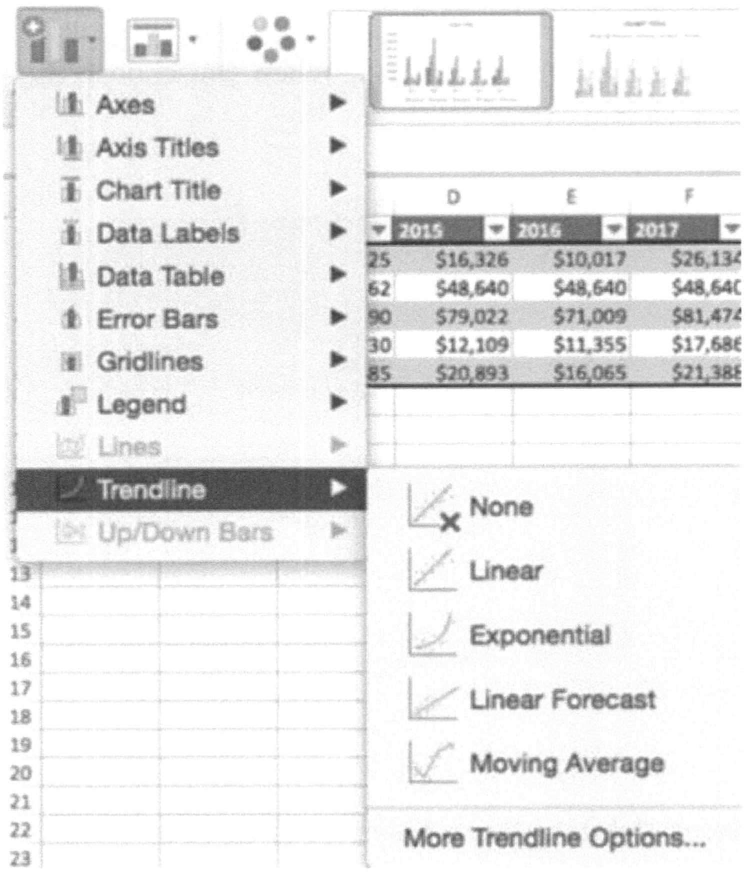

Excel provides the trendline for every commodity if you're evaluating five different goods over time. Click on Product A and then the blue OK key to build the product's linear trendlines.

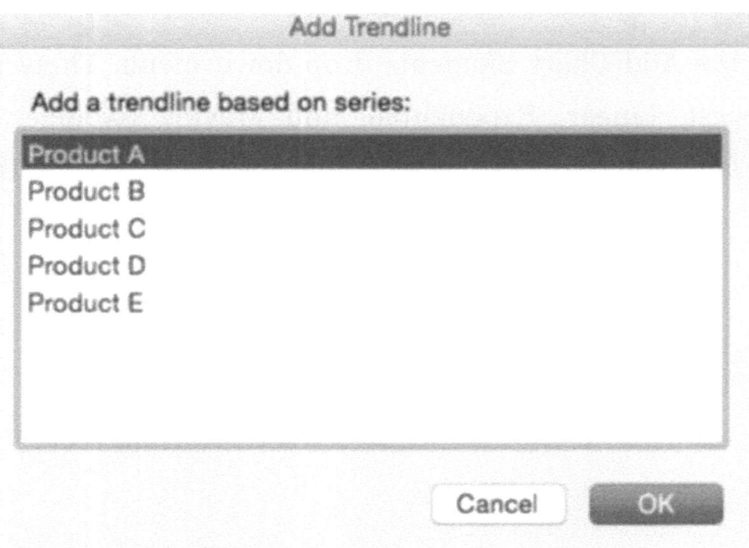

The dotted trendlines will now appear on your chart to reflect the linear progression of Product A. The words "Linear (Product A)" has now been added to the legend.

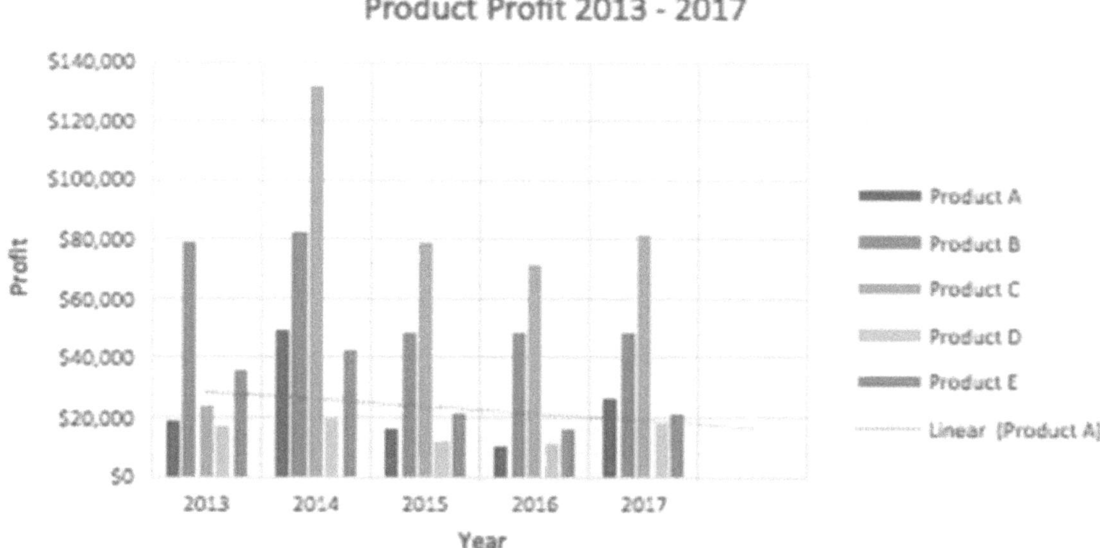

Double-click on Trendlines to see a trendline equation in your chart. On the right-hand side of the screen, a Format Trendlines window will appear. At the bottom of the window, check the box beside the Display equation in the chart. The equation is now visible on the chart.

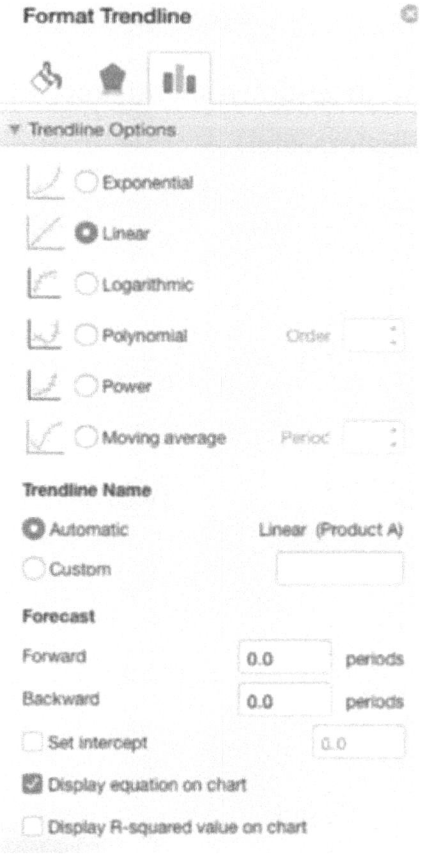

Note: You can make as many trendlines as you like with each attribute in the chart. Here's an illustration of a chart of trendlines for Products A and C.

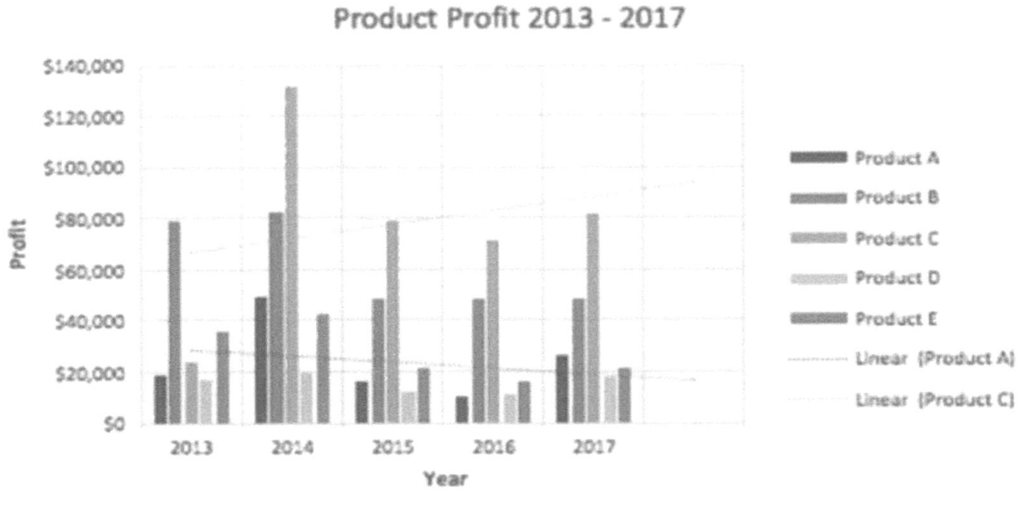

Up/Down Bars cannot be used in the column chart, yet they can be used in line charts to display rises and declines in data points.

Adjust a Quick Layout

Quick Layout is the toolbar's second drop-down menu, and it helps you easily adjust the layout of items in the chart (legends, titles, clusters, etc.).

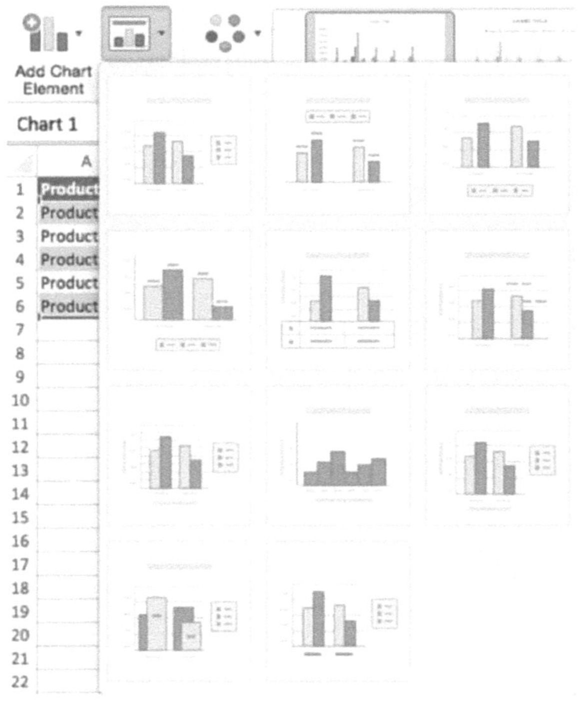

There are eleven quick layout choices. Hover the cursor over these various choices for a description, then choose what you need to use.

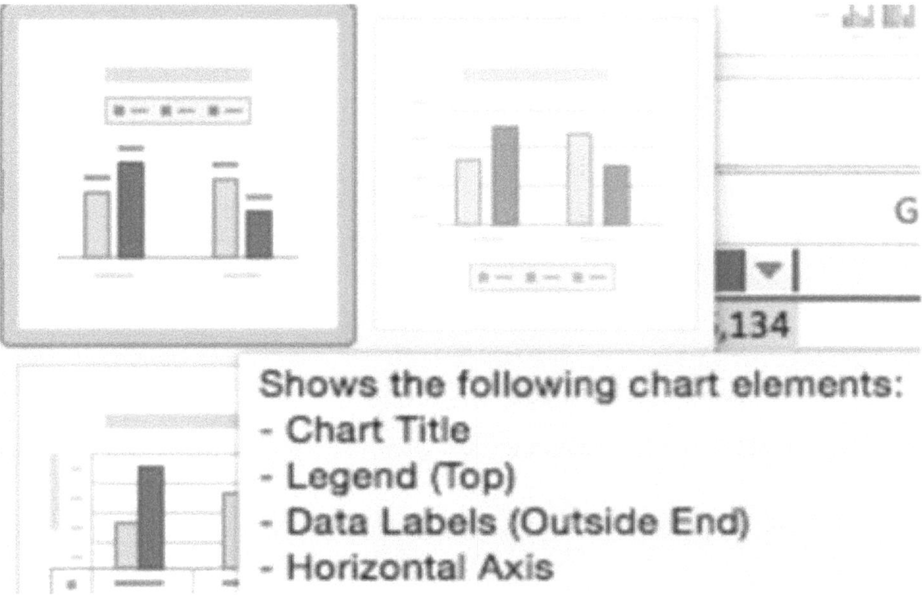

Change the Colors

Change Colors in the next drop-down menu in the toolbar. Choose the color scheme that best suits your needs (these can be aesthetic and complement the colors and theme of your brand).

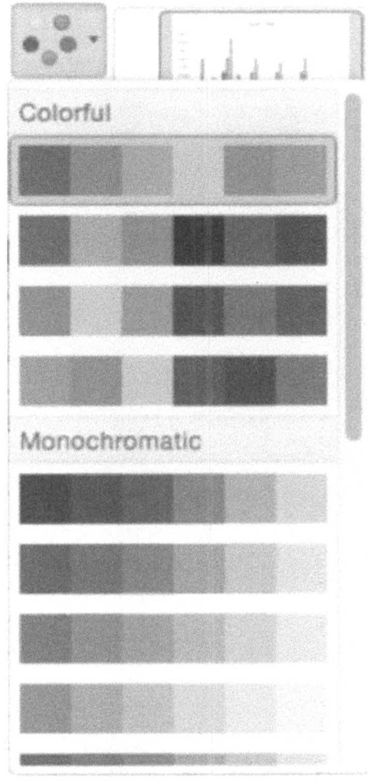

Change the Style

There are fourteen chart forms used for the charts (cluster column). The chart will be shown in Style 1 by default; however, you can adjust it. To see further choices, click the arrow to the right of the picture bar.

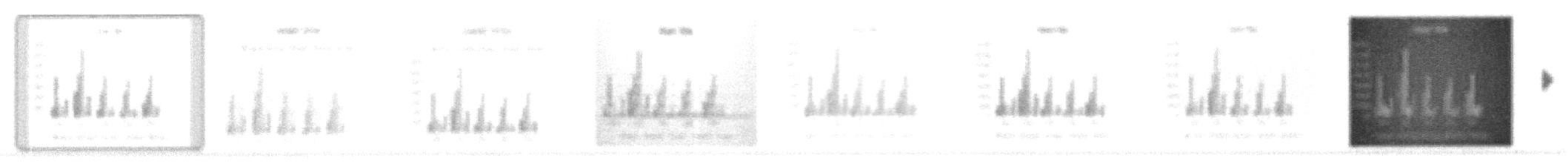

Switch Column/Row

To rotate the axes, click the Switch Row/Column button on your toolbar. Notice that flipping axes for each chart often isn't useful, for instance, if you have more than two variables.

Switching the column and row, in this case, flips the product and year (profit remains on the y-axis). The graph is now organized by product (rather than by year), and a color-coded legend corresponds to a year (not a product). To avoid doubt, go to the legend and change the Series to the actual years.

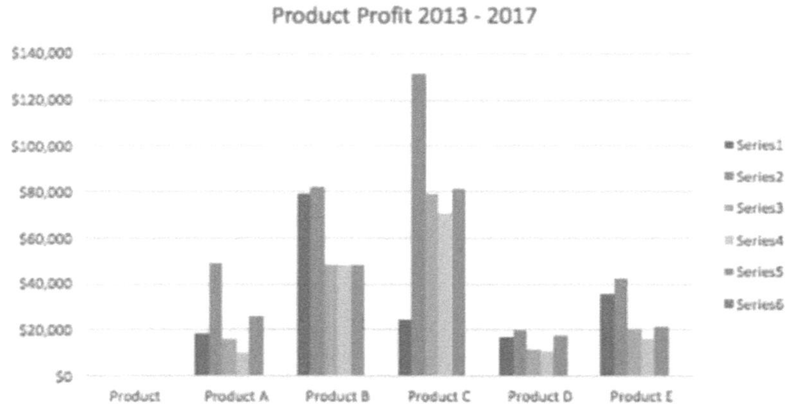

Select the Data

To adjust the context of your files, click the Select Data button on the toolbar.

A window opens. Click the Ok button after typing in the cell set you want. This latest data set is reflected in the table automatically.

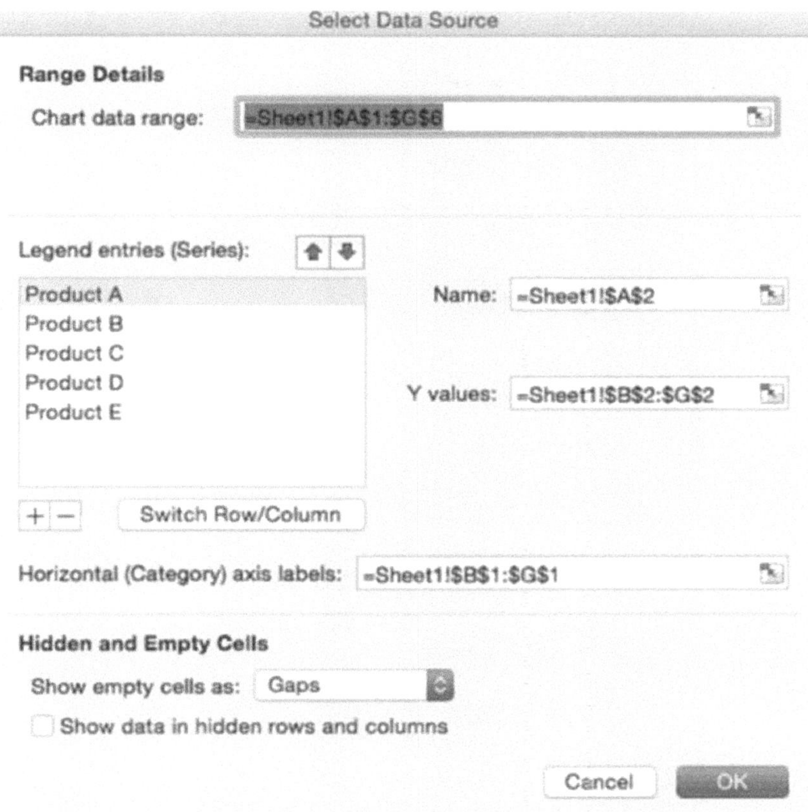

Change the Chart Type

Change a chart type from the drop-down menu.

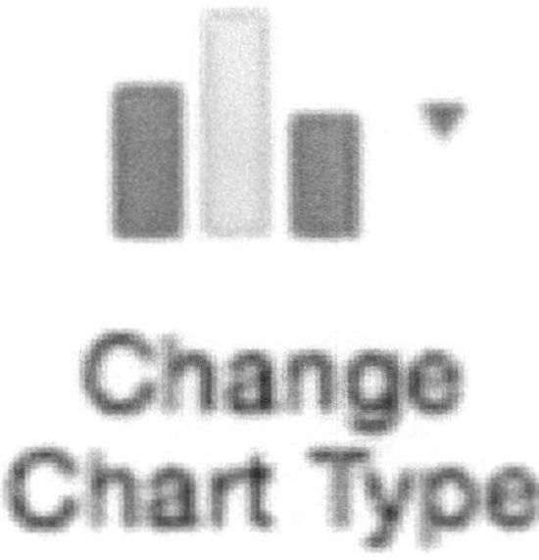

Here, you can adjust the chart category to each of Excel's nine chart types. It is essential to double-check that the data is suitable for the chart format you've chosen.

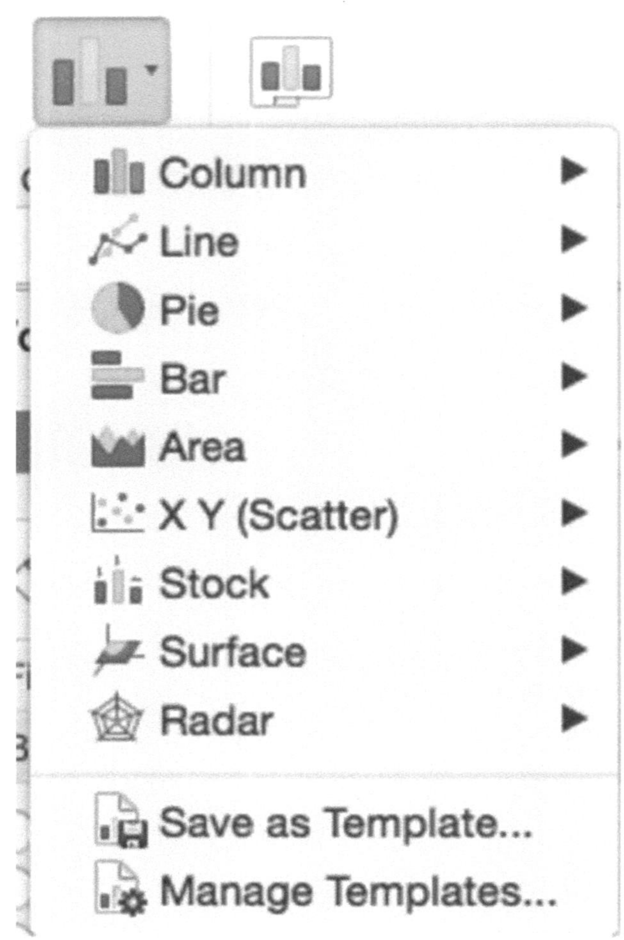

By pressing Save as Template..., you can save the chart as a template.

You'll be presented with the dialog box in which you can give your design a name. Excel can automatically generate a folder for the models to organize documents efficiently. To save your work, click the Save icon.

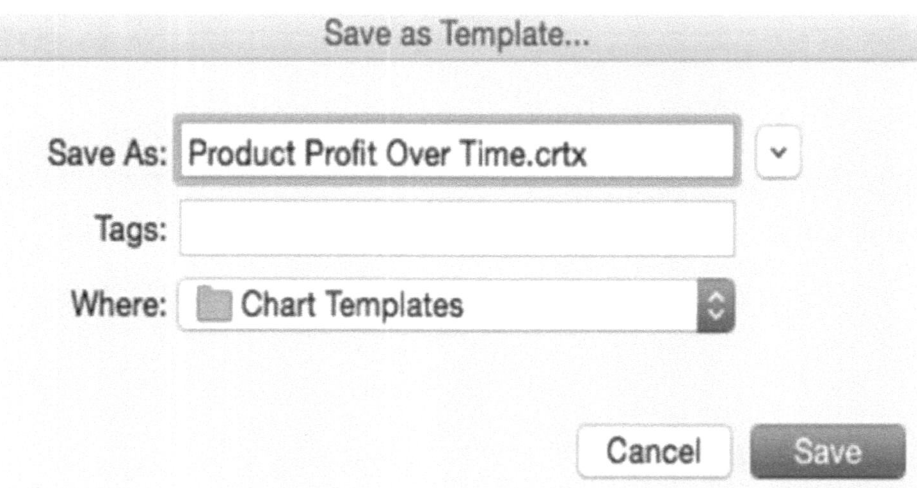

Move a Chart

On the far right of your toolbar, click the Move Chart button.

You'll see a discussion box in which you can select where to put the chart. You can either use this box to make a new layer (New sheet) or use it as an entity in another sheet. To continue, press the blue OK key.

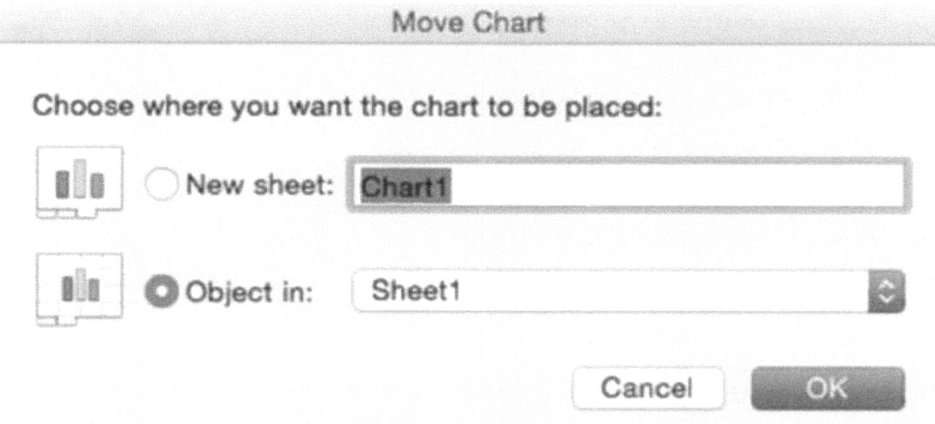

Change the Formatting

You can adjust the colors, scale, design, fill, and orientation of all components and text in a chart, as well as insert shapes using the Format tab. To have a chart represent your company's brand or style, go to the Format tab and use an available shortcut (images, colors, etc.).

Select the chart feature you want to update from the drop-down menu on the top-left of your toolbar.

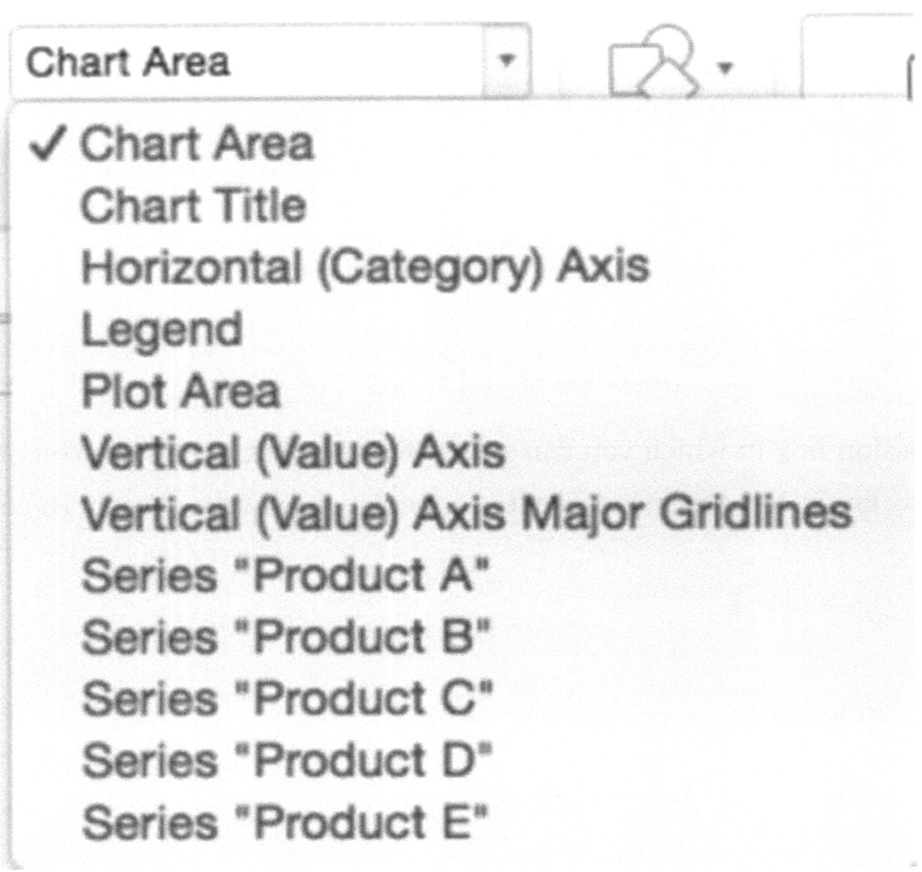

Delete a Chart

Simply choose a chart and press the Delete button on the keyboard to delete it.

How You Can Make the Graph Using Excel

Although graphs and charts are two different features, Excel groups all graphs into the chart categories mentioned in previous sections. Follow the steps below and choose the right graph form to generate a graph or another type of chart.

- To make a graph with workbook data, select a range

- By moving your cursor over cells that hold data you want to include in a graph, you will highlight them.

- The grayed-out cell contents will be illuminated.

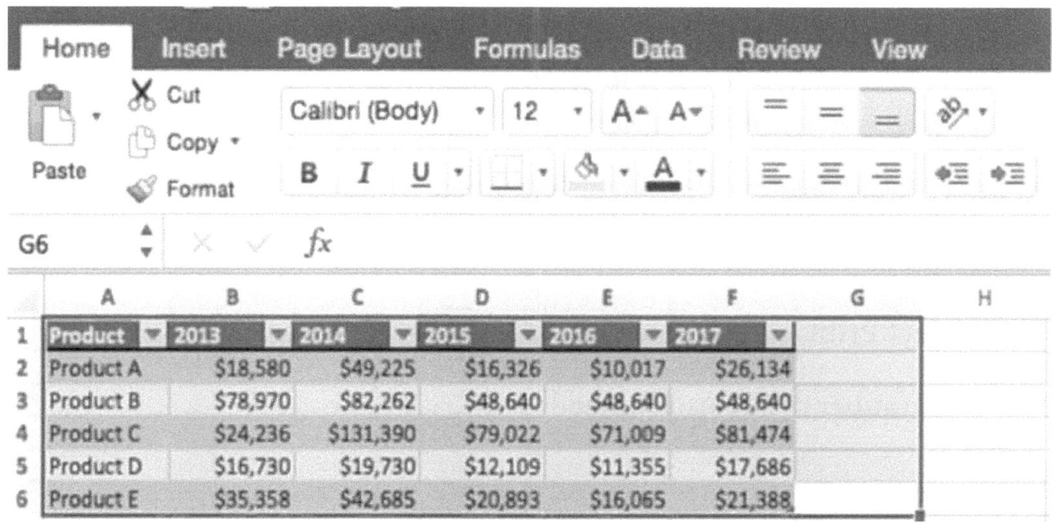

- After the text has been outlined, you can choose a graph (Excel refers to a chart).

- On the toolbar, choose Recommended Charts from your Insert tab. Then choose the graph form you want to use.

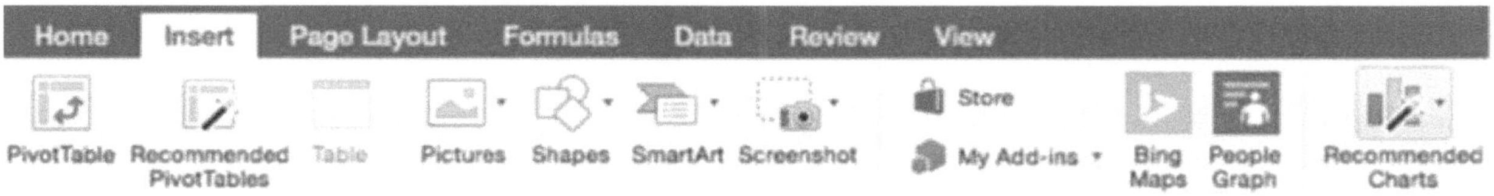

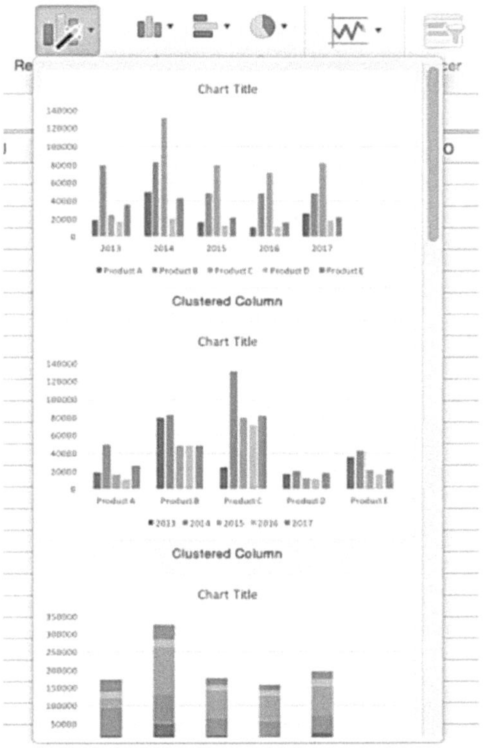

You now have the graph on your screen. To personalize your graph, repeat the measures outlined in the previous section. When making a graph, all the functions for making a chart remain the same.

1.59.2 Printing Charts

Select the desired chart within your cookbook

Click on File then select Print

Set your printer and number of copies you need

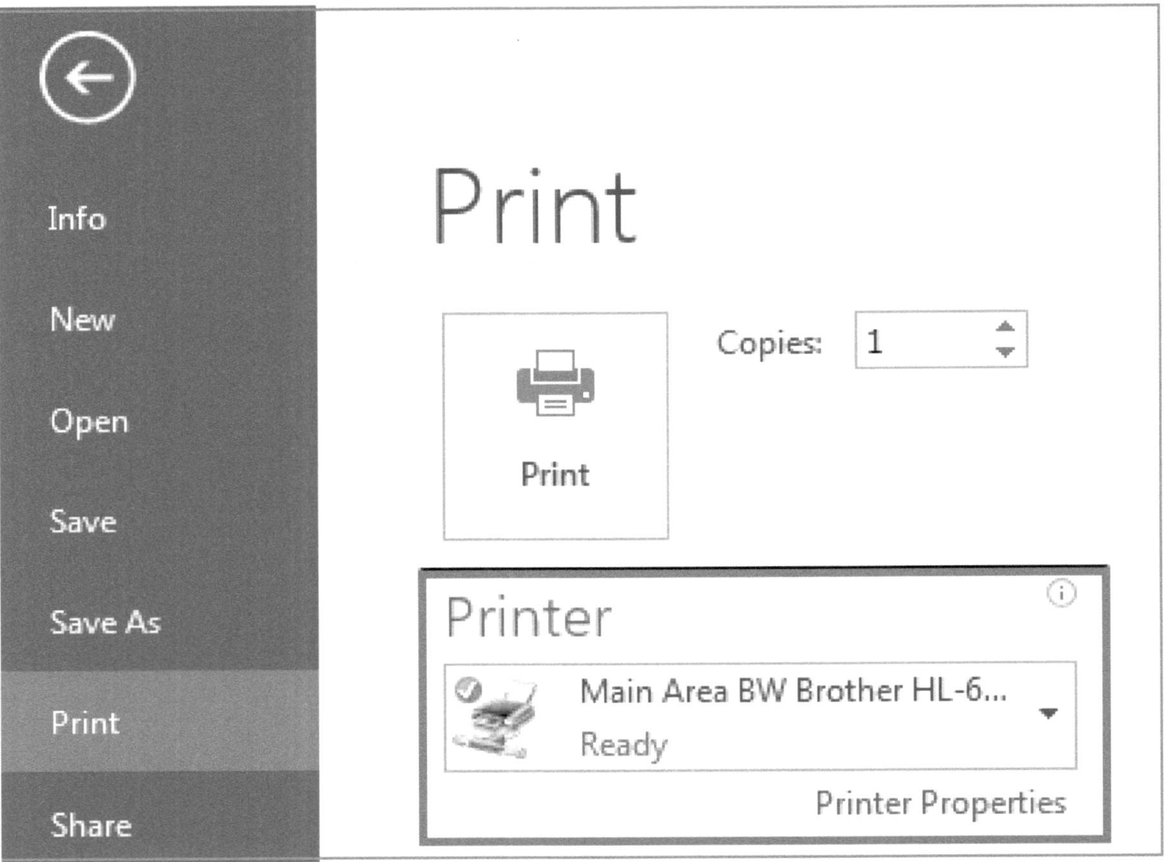

Click the Print Icon

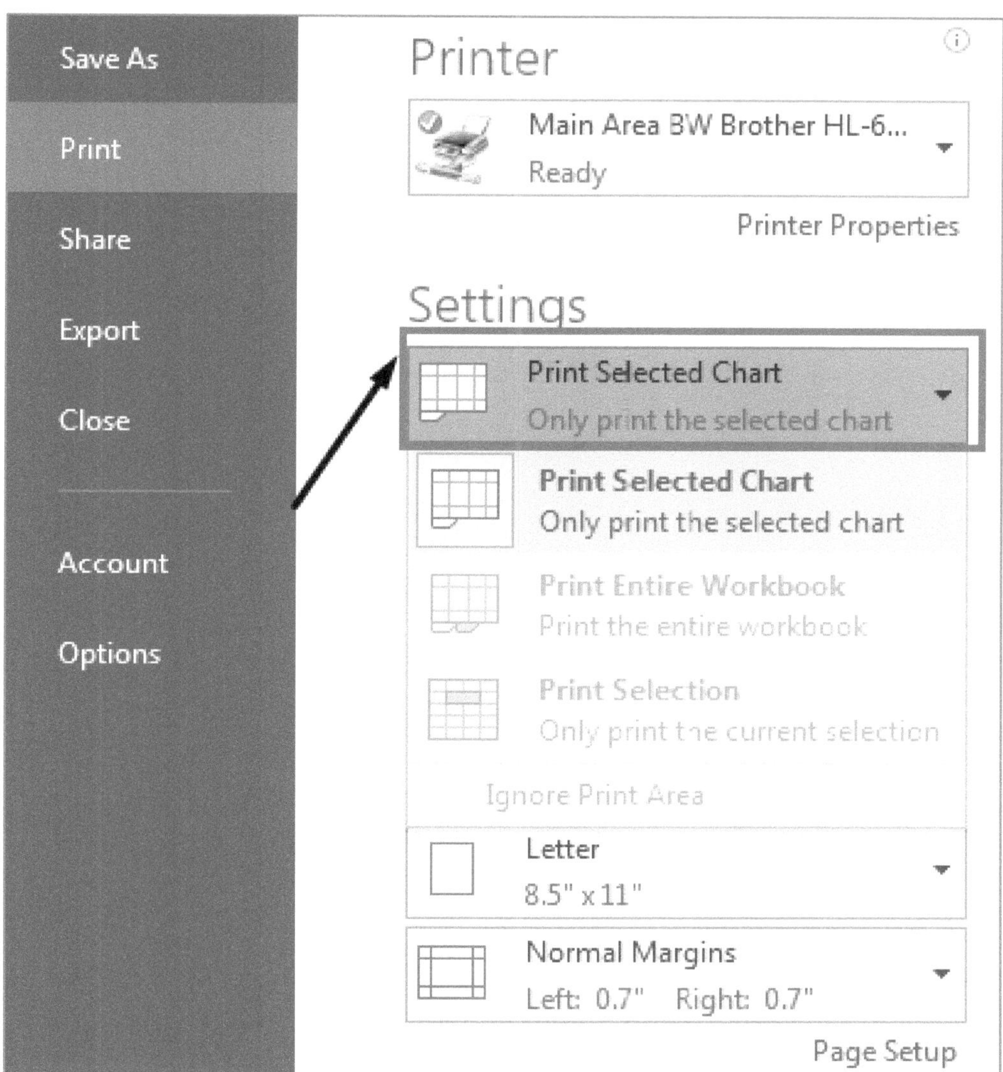

1.60 Types of Graphs

Knowing which types of graphs to create with Microsoft Excel can make a huge difference to the look of your presentation. Excel has all the tools you need to create a truly impressive presentation, from bar graphs to line graphs. Learn how to create these types of graphs with MS Excel today. The possibilities are endless! Try out these simple tips, and you'll be on your way to creating visually stunning presentations!

Column Graphs

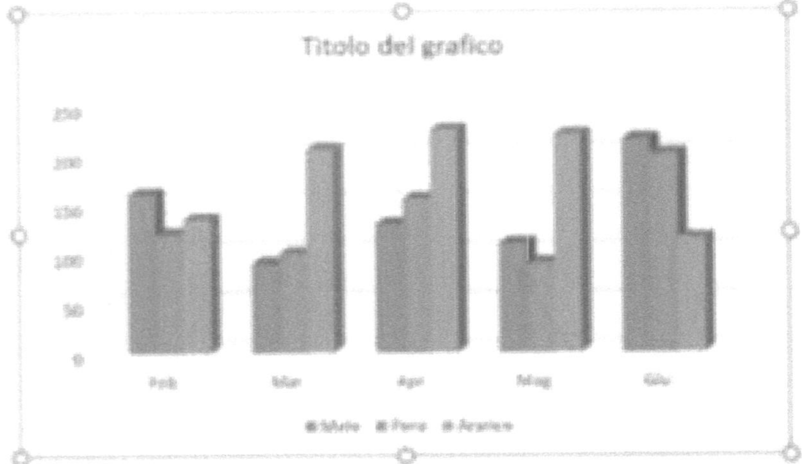

To design a column chart within Excel, you'll take the following steps:

Highlight the information you wish to use in the column chart. We picked the range A1:C7 for this case.

Select the Insert button from the toolbar at the top of each page. Click a chart from its drop-down menu by pressing the Excel Column chart option within Charts Category. For this case, we went with the first column chart in the 2-D Column section (regarded as Clustered Column).

All sales and expense statistics will be reflected in the column chart in the rectangle bar spreadsheet. Vertical blue lines represent sales values, while vertical orange lines represent costs. For certain vertical lines, their values of axes could be seen along the left side of the graph.

Last but not least, let's alter the column chart's explanation.

Click the "Chart Title" link towards the top of a graphic item to adjust the title. One ought to be able to notice that the title can be changed. Put the text you want to appear as the title here.

Line Graphs

To create a line graph in MS Excel, start by highlighting the data in two columns. Then, select the option to "Insert Line Graph. " Then, click "OK. " The line graph will appear on the spreadsheet. You can also change the title text to make it stand out. Finally, select the "Line" option to add a border to the text. After selecting a title for your line graph, you can change its color and style.

You can customize a line graph by adding diverse types of markers. You can also add annotations to it and connect it to certain points. You can then copy the chart to PowerPoint or Word. However, make sure to select the "Insert Shapes" check box before inserting any shapes. Otherwise, the shape will not show up in the chart image. Similarly, you can change the color of the line by clicking on the legend.

A line graph is a great way to analyze trends over time. You can also use it to compare two or more variables over time. A line graph can also help you detect relationships between variables. However, when viewed over large datasets, lines can become clumsy, therefore it is not recommended for continuous variables. Line graphs in MS Excel have a variety of options to suit your needs. You can choose to create a single line graph, a multiple line chart, or both.

Bar Graphs

You can format the bar graphs in MS Excel using the Format button. You can also hide or edit the title and other elements of the graph. The bar graph appears after you click OK. Right-click on the graph and choose Format Data Series to edit the title and other elements. A pane appears where you choose Fill & Line option or Varying colors by point. Right-click on the plot area to edit it.

Click the axis in which you want to plot data. The axis label will be on the bottom of the graph. Click the axis title to change it. You can also change the colors of the axis. You can choose different colors for the axis by clicking on the axis and changing the styles. Click the axis and adjust the color of the data clusters to fit the theme.

Bar graphs are used to present data that represents frequencies or certain categories. To create a bar graph, you first need to enter data in the spreadsheet. To select all data, click the A1 cell and the bottom value of the B column. You can also select different column types by selecting the top-left and bottom-right cells of the data group. Then, select the "Bar chart" icon within the Charts group. The icon looks like a sequence of 3 vertical bars.

1.61 Creating Charts in Excel

Charts are a fantastic tool for graphically communicating facts and information with others. The data that is represented in charts serves as their foundation. In order to create a chart, the first and most important step is to choose the relevant data to display. To begin, you must input your information into Excel. You may highlight cells in your graph by dragging your mouse over the cells that contain the information you want to use in your graph. After inputting your data and choosing a cell range, you will be able to pick the chart type that will be used to represent your data.

Consider the following scenario: you have a spreadsheet with two data columns. The variable Year is located in column A, while the variable Value is located in column B. You want to

create a chart where the variable Value is shown on the vertical axis and the year is plotted on the horizontal.

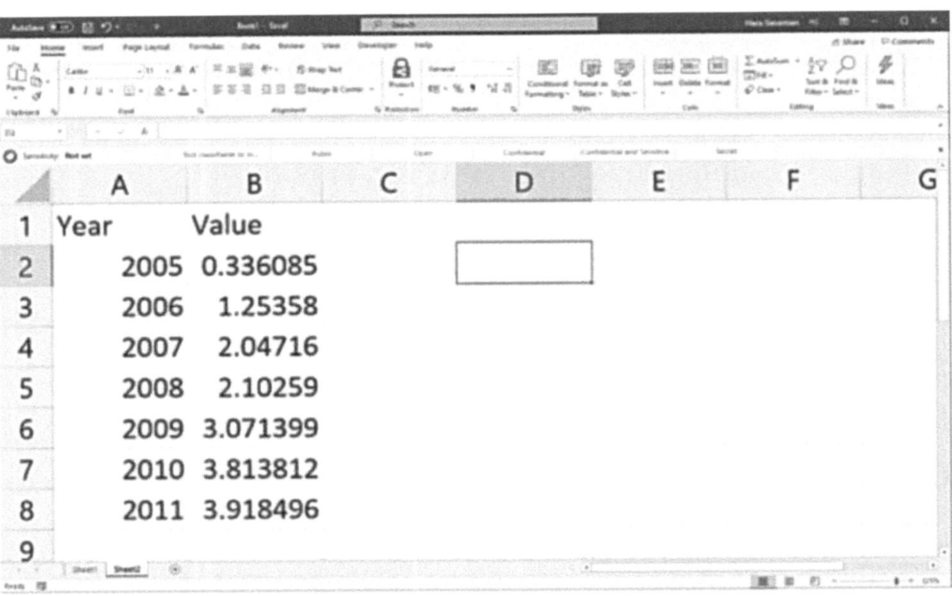

After selecting your data for the chart, follow the steps shown below to incorporate the chart into your spreadsheet.

1. Decide which information you want to utilize and why.

2. Choose the Insert tab from the ribbon's drop-down menu.

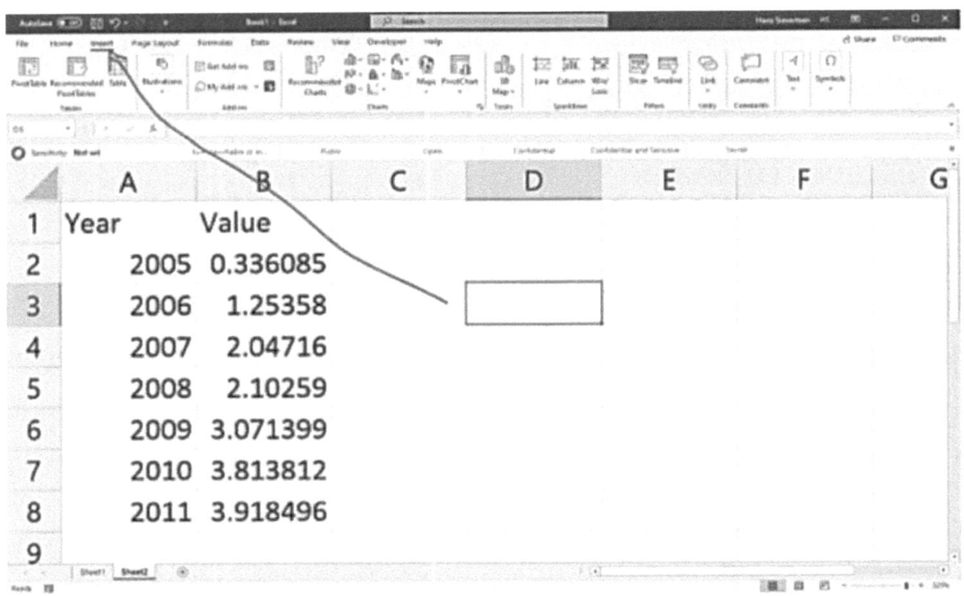

3. On the ribbon, select Insert Chart.

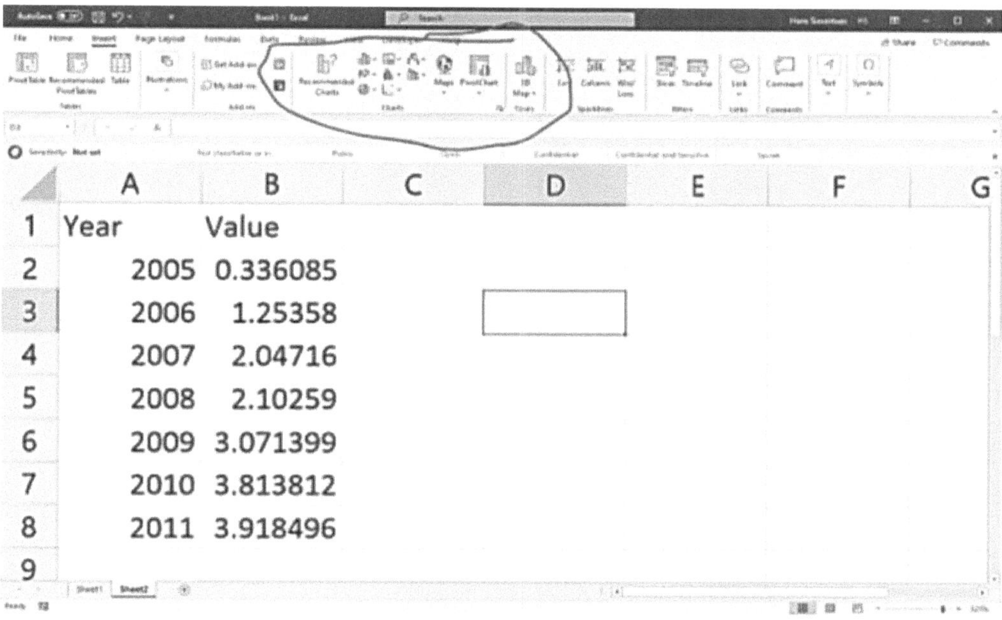

4. Go via the Chart settings and choose Show Previews to see the previews.

5. Please choose the appropriate chart and click on it to insert it. The line chart shown in the following graphic is utilized.

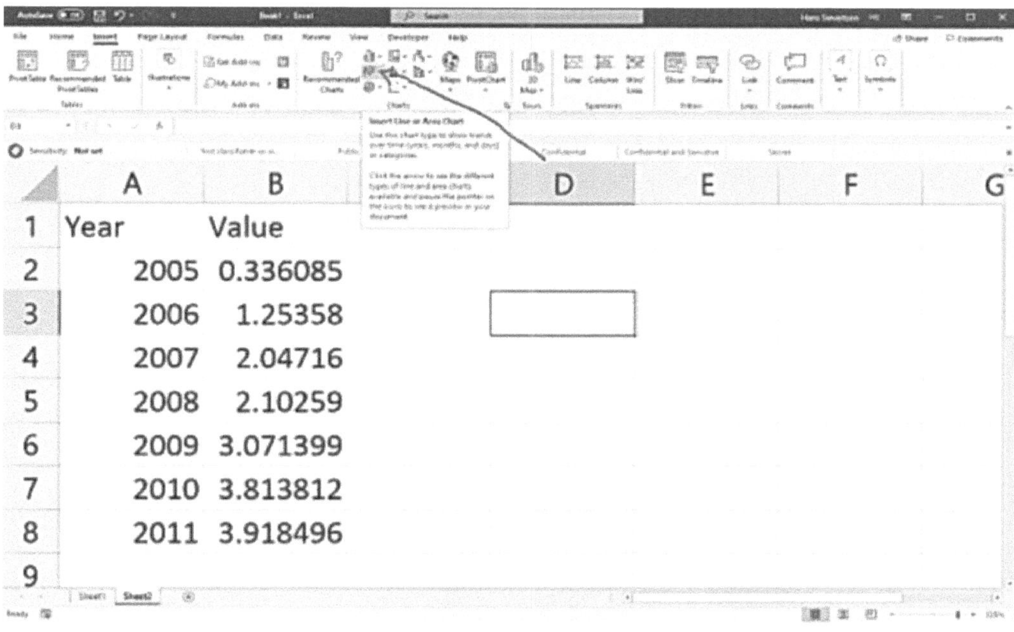

6. When you click on the line chart icon, a drop-down menu with other chart kinds is displayed.

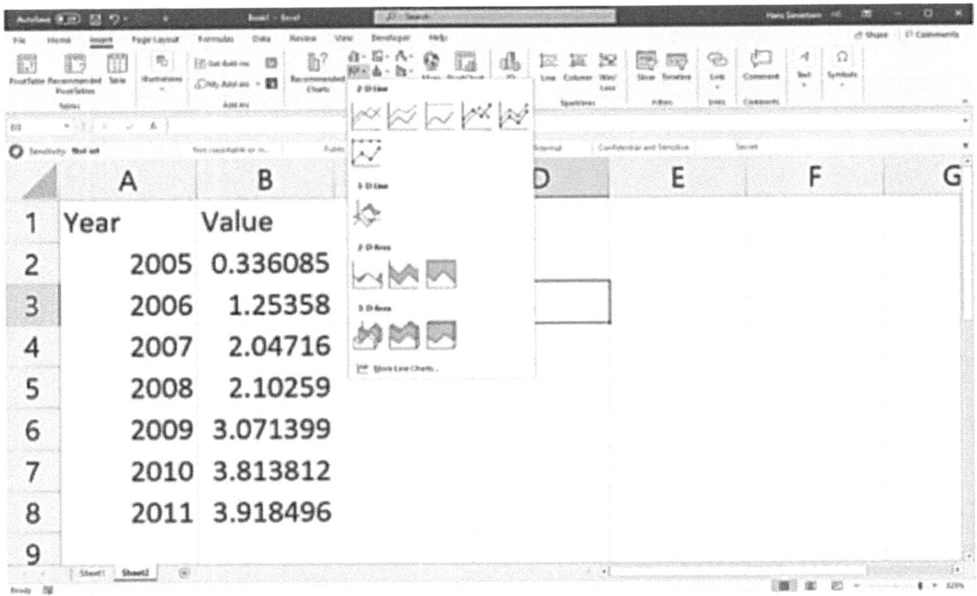

7. To begin creating the chart, you must first tell Excel what data to use as a starting point. Following the selection of the chart canvas (which may be accomplished by just clicking on it), go to the "Chart Design" menu and choose "Select Data" (see below). Alternatively, you may right-click on the graph and pick "Select Data" from the context menu.

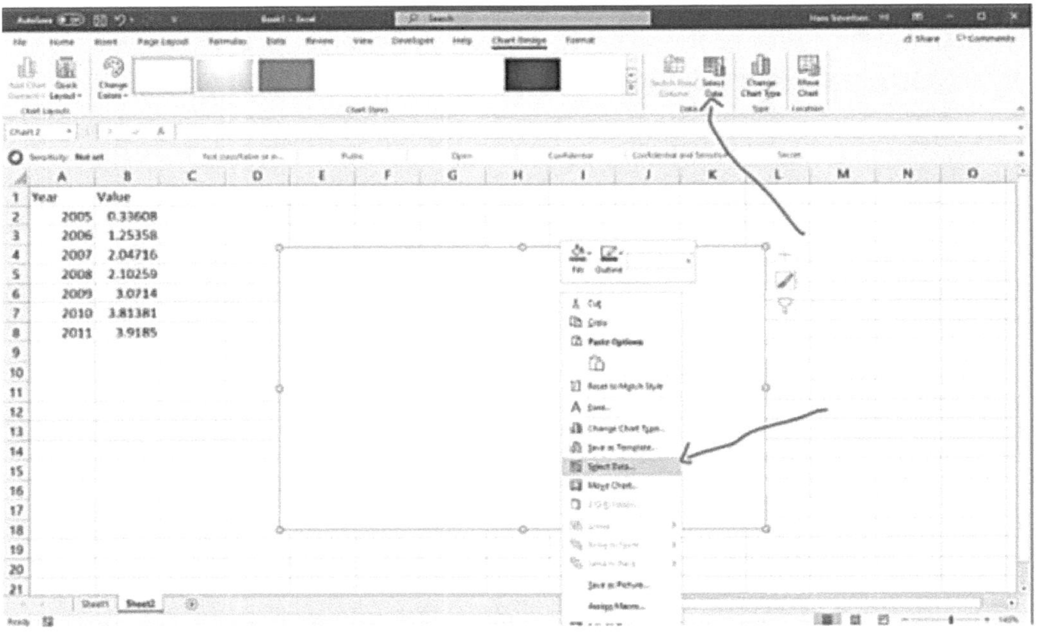

8. The data selection options are shown in the menu below. You can select the whole data area to be utilized at the top. You have the option of selecting which data to show on the vertical axis (y-axis) of the left panel and which variable to display on the horizontal axis (x-axis) of the right panel (x-axis).

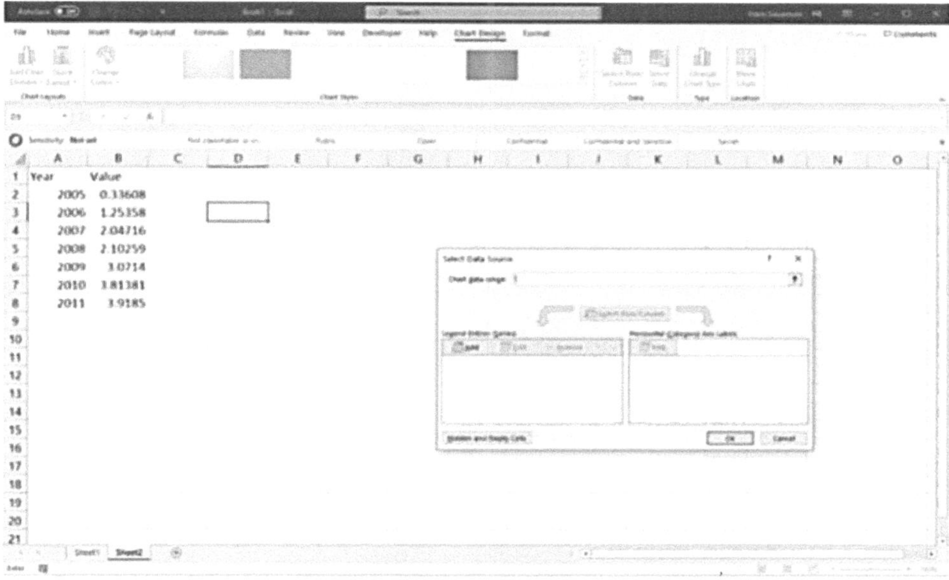

9. Let's tell Excel what data to utilize for the vertical axis first. As indicated below, click "Add."

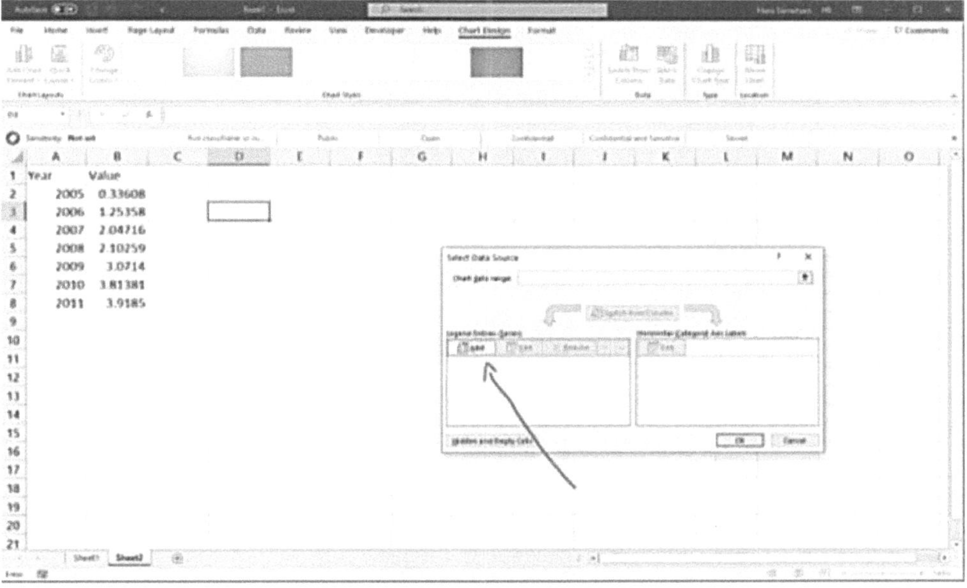

10. A menu, similar to the one seen below should now be shown. Fill in the blanks with a title and a description of the series' content. In the "Series name" column, you can manually enter the description of the series.

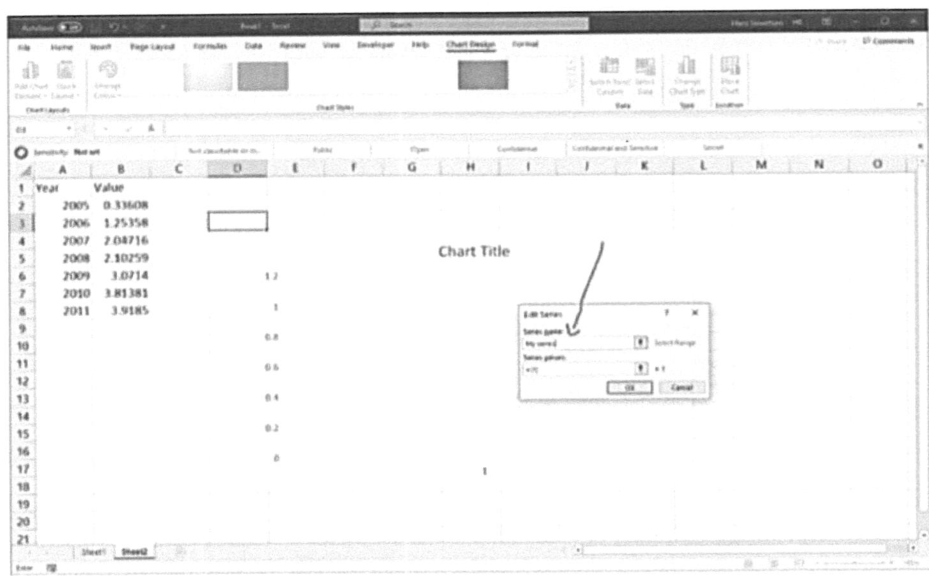

11. For the "Series Values," click the arrow up icon. Select all of the cells containing the values you want to display on the vertical axis.

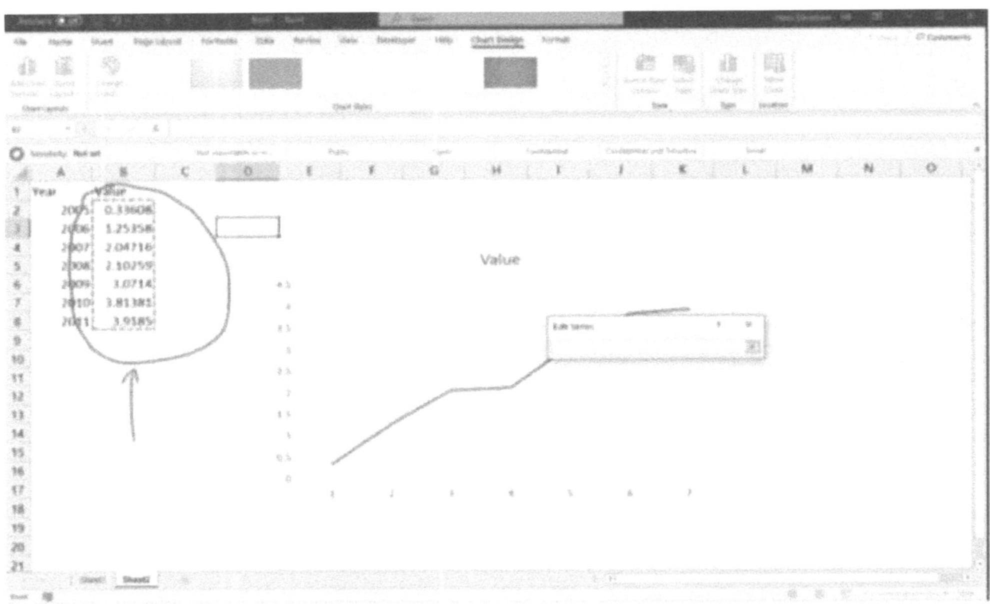

12. The series for the horizontal axis may be selected by selecting "Edit" from the right-hand panel. Select the data for the horizontal axis using the same strategy as you did for the vertical axis, and then click the OK button to finish.

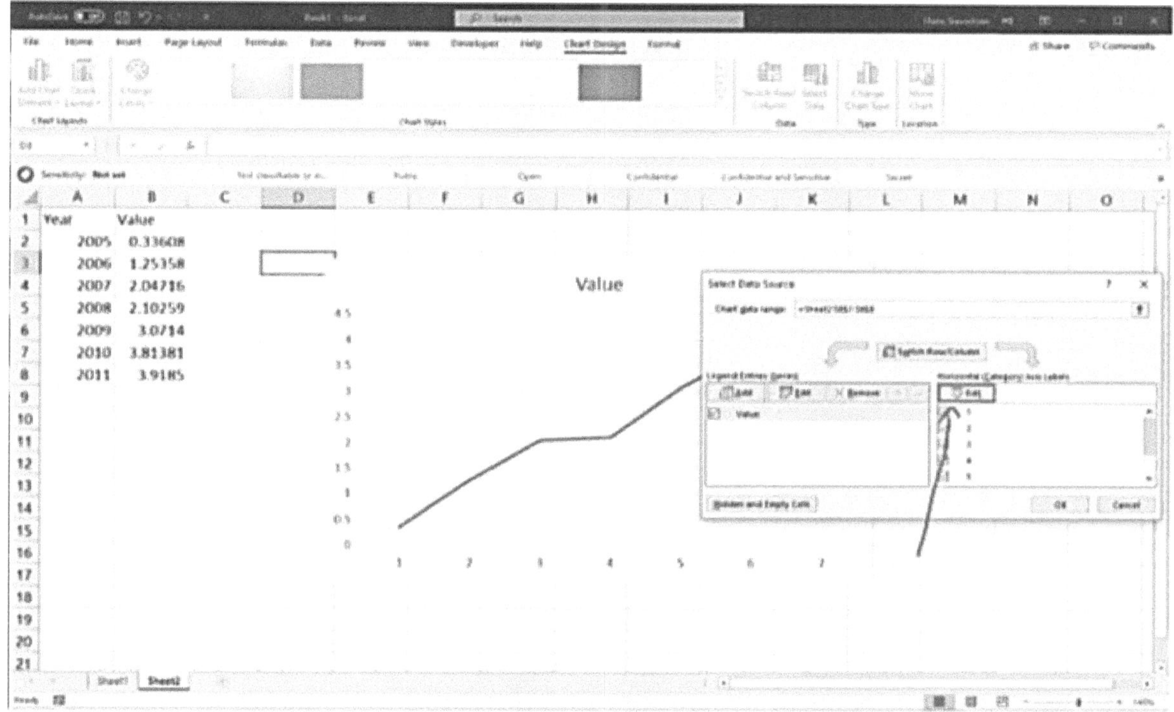

13. To complete the "Select Data" operation, click "OK."

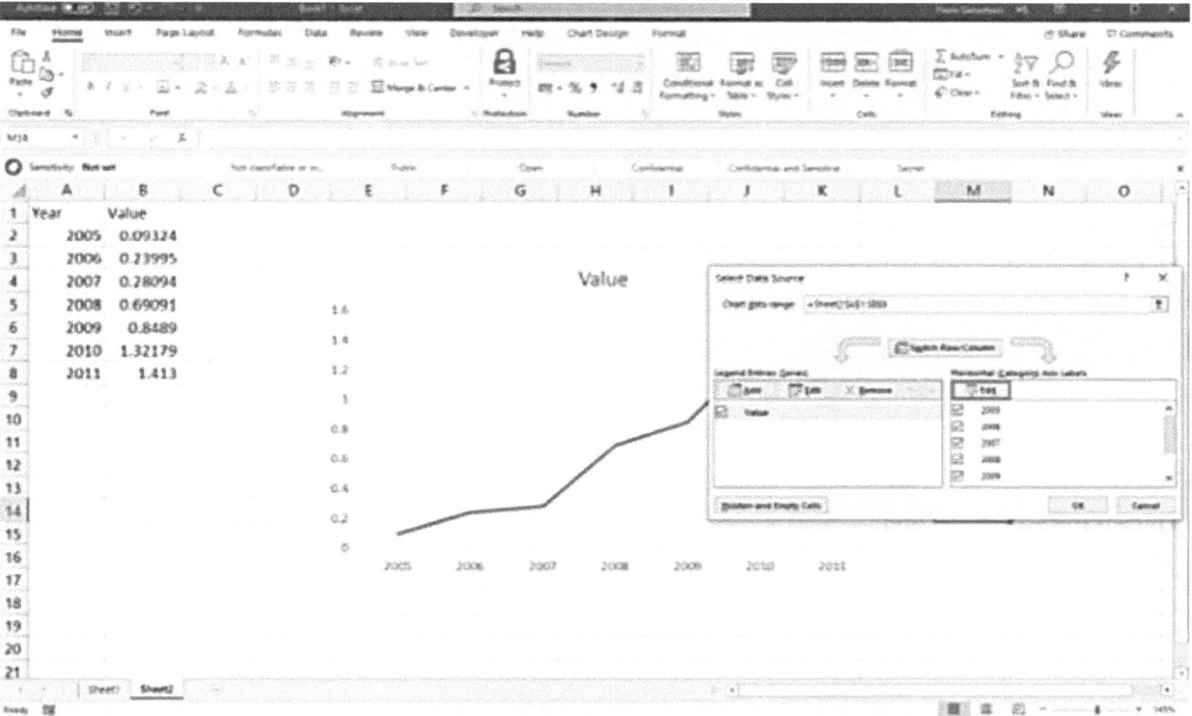

14. Your Chart will be inserted.

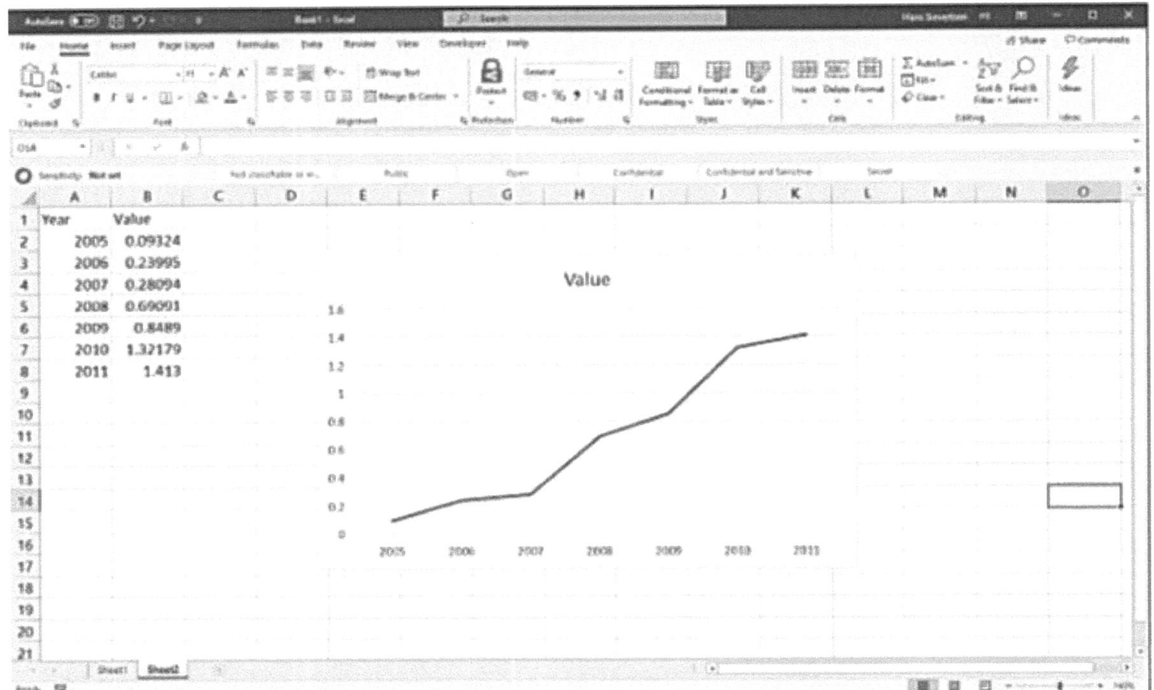

1.62 Create an Excel Table

You are ready to create the formatted Table after you have organized the data as mentioned above.

• Select a cell from the data list you prepared.

• Click the Insert tab from the Ribbon.

• Select the Table command from the Tables group.

• The range for your data should appear automatically in the Create Table dialogue box, and the My table has headers option should be checked. You can change the range and check the box if necessary.

• To accept these settings, click OK.

Pivot Table In MS Excel

You probably already know what a Pivot Table is, but are you sure you know how to use it? Read on to learn more about this helpful tool! Pivot tables let you easily compare and contrast data. Its most useful feature is its ability to visualize data in different ways. Its flexibility is the most compelling reason to use it. You can even create your own custom Pivot Tables. Fortunately, it's incredibly easy to create these tables!

1.63 What are Pivot Tables?

Pivot tables in MS Excel allow you to analyze your data in a variety of ways. You can use them to identify trends, compare data across categories, or make a report of the results of an analysis. This feature allows you to make changes to the data without affecting the original export. You should always save your work before making changes so that you can return to the previous version of the file later.

To create a pivot table, open a worksheet with data you would like to analyze. Choose the New Worksheet option. Choose a location for the table in the worksheet. Click the Location box to select the first cell of data. Alternatively, select an existing worksheet. You can also select the Existing Worksheet option and place the pivot table on that worksheet. You can also choose to select a cell with data that already exists.

Pivot tables in MS Excel can summarize data from thousands of rows. Once you create a pivot table, you can choose to save it or reuse it in another Excel workbook. In the XLSX file, you can also reuse existing pivot tables. Be sure to rename them according to the date they were exported. By doing this, you can avoid wasting time creating multiple worksheets. You can also use an existing Excel file with the same data if you need to change the layout of the pivot table.

1.64 Why are Pivot Tables Important?

The basic idea behind Pivot Tables is to compare a single data table with multiple ones. Pivot Tables contain columns of data that are ordered based on their field names. You can easily compare Pivot Tables by dragging and dropping fields from one column to another. These fields will automatically update the Pivot Table in the worksheet. There are many options for report layout, including redundant ones.

The data in a pivot table is referred to as the Source Data. The data is either contained in the worksheet or is sourced from an external database. Pivot Tables are useful when you want to summarize thousands of rows of data. You can drag and drop fields to populate the values. Then, when you need to change a field's value, just drag and drop the data into the corresponding field and click "update" or "refresh" to get the updated information.

Another benefit of pivot tables is that they are easy to create. They don't require complex formulas, and you can set them up in minutes. That means less work and faster results. Organize the source data properly before starting the process to make pivot tables. A well-designed pivot table can help you avoid redundancies and make your analysis more accurate. And as you can see, there are many benefits to using them in your work with Excel.

1.65 Creating Pivot Tables

Pivot tables can be used to get all of the data together while still allowing you to process and sort it in various ways. Tick the beside the field name to build a PivotTable, and right-click the field name to select a place to shift the object to (i.e., Add to Column Labels, Add to Row Labels, Add to Report Filter, and Add to Values).

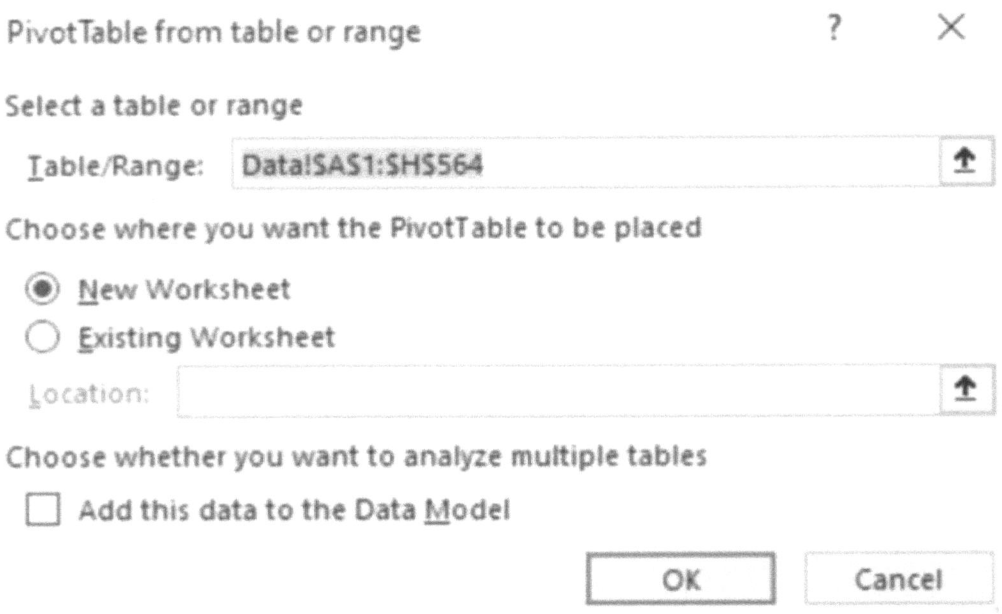

You may also move an object from the Pivot Table Category List to one of the fields below by clicking on each field name, keeping down the cursor, and moving it to one of the fields below.

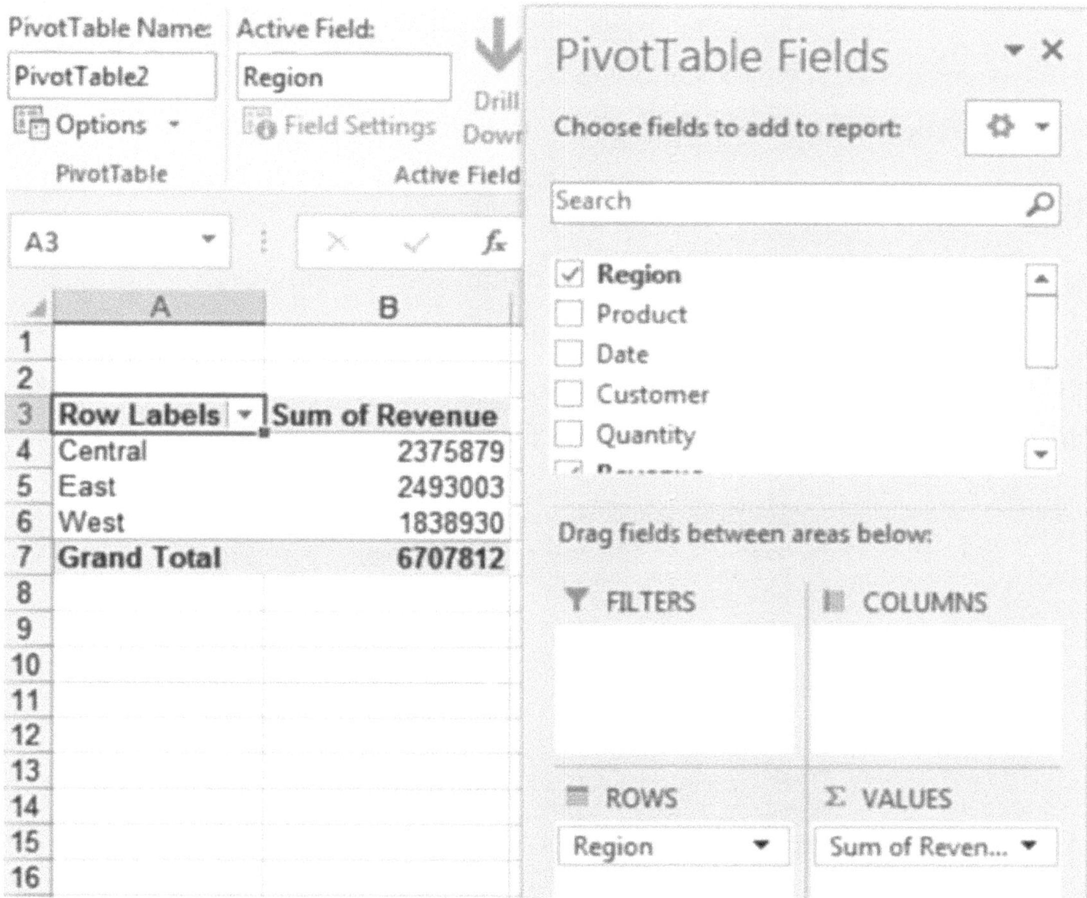

The most interesting thing to note regarding Pivot Tables is that they allow you to generate relevant data without picking and entering manually. Keep in mind that any modifications you make can often be undone if you later discover they aren't necessary.

A PivotTable Field List disappears when you click outside the layout region (of a PivotTable report). Click within the PivotTable layout region or report to restore the field list.

Using class as an example, you'll use the Pivot Table you just generated to add a few of the essential fields to columns and rows so you can start working with the results. Type Topic in the Rows field, and Ex. Teacher and Ex. Course in the Values field.

The information in the Subject area is automatically displayed as rows on the left side of a report. The data in Ex. Course and Ex. The teacher, which includes figures, appears accurately in a right-hand field. It will show us the number of these fields for every subject matter. Click the downward arrow in front of each value in the fields array, Values > >Value Field Settings >> Average, or right-click the column title inside the PivotTable to adjust this to average. It's worth noting that you have many options to choose from.

Click PivotTable Analyze Behavior >> Actions party >> Clear >> Clear Everything on the Ribbon to restart the report and delete all the fields so you can start again.

1.66 Sorting Data

Sort the data using different parameters, such as name, value, count, or other criteria, as the basic pivot table is in place. Click the auto-sort option and then "additional sort options" to select various criteria to sort the data. Another alternative is to right-click anywhere around the table and choose Sort, then "additional sort options " from the menu.

Date	Channel	Product	Revenue	Shipping Cost	Marketing Cost
1/1/2018	Facebook	T-shirt	45	-5	-3
1/1/2018	Email	Pants	75	-5	-8
1/1/2018	LinkedIn	Hat	25	-2	-8
1/1/2018	Email	Shorts	35	-3	0
1/1/2018	Twitter	Pants	75	-5	-12
1/1/2018	AdWords	Shorts	35	-3	-8
1/1/2018	Instagram	T-shirt	45	-5	-4
1/1/2018	Snapchat	T-shirt	45	-5	-2
1/2/2018	Facebook	T-shirt	45	-5	-16
1/2/2018	LinkedIn	Shorts	35	-3	-9
1/2/2018	Email	Pants	75	-5	0
1/2/2018	Twitter	Hat	25	-2	-3
1/2/2018	AdWords	Shorts	35	-3	-1
1/2/2018	Instagram	Pants	75	-5	-4

In MS Excel, sorting data rearranges the rows depending on the contents of a certain column. Sorting a table to place names in alphabetical order is a good idea. Alternatively, you might arrange data by amount from smallest to greatest or from biggest to smallest.

Here's an example of a table with carelessly organized records. The states aren't in alphabetical order, and the months aren't in chronological order.

Let's start by sorting the data by state alphabetically. The steps for sorting a table are outlined below. Choose the table, then select *Sort* and *Filter* from the Home menu. A sorting dialogue box appears.

This dialogue box enables you to add more than one level of sorting to the usual one. In the Sort by box, choose *State* and *A to Z* in the Order box. The final product is what you see below.

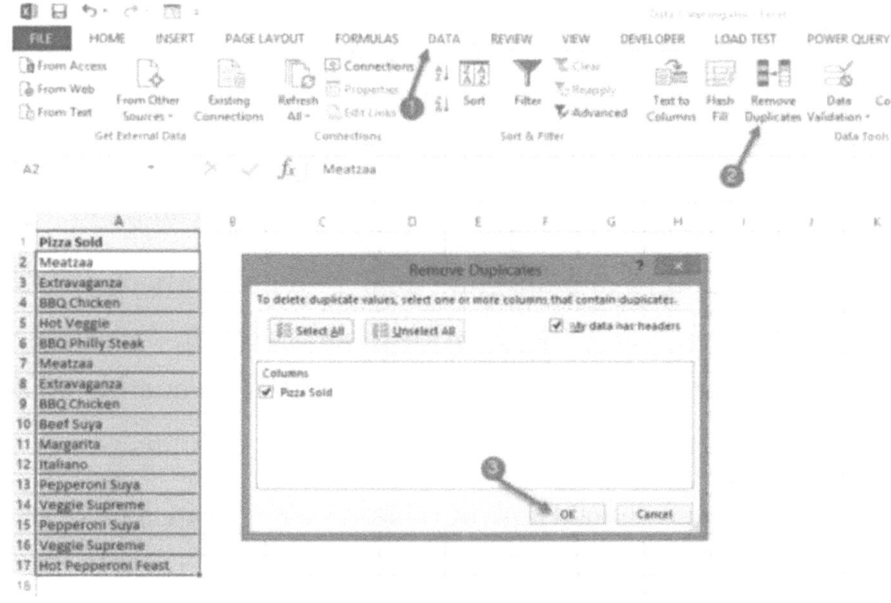

In the sorting dialogue box, you may add an additional level of sorting. This would be beneficial for sorting tables such as those used in national population censuses. You may choose to arrange by state first (from Abia to Zamfara) and then by Local Government Areas. As a result, you'll have a configuration similar to the one shown below. The next step is to arrange the months in the natural sequence we are used to—January to December. This will need a form of sorting known as "Left to Right," as opposed to the "Top to Bottom" sorting we just completed.

1.67 Filtering Data

Adding a filter to the data is a simple method to sort it. With the filter feature, we may see data for particular sub-sections with a single click. An additional box appears at the top of the pivot table, indicating the filter has been applied by dragging the desired category from the list of choices down to the Filters section.

The filter feature is one of Excel users' most often used tools. It lets you pick what parts of a table you wish to see and conceal the rest.

It's straightforward to use and can be accessed from three distinct Excel locations. Filter may be accessed by right-clicking and choosing *Filter*, Selecting *Sort* and *Filter* from the Home menu, and clicking the Data dropdown menu. You'll notice a dropdown box beside the table headings after you've switched on the Filter tool by clicking on it. By selecting the dropdown box, you may see all of the unique items in that area and choose which ones you wish to see (hiding the rest). All things are chosen by default, so you'll have to deselect the ones you don't want to view. Aside from the BBQ Chicken, all other pizza toppings were left unselected in the screenshot below (meaning only BBQ Chicken was selected). The blue row numbers are Excel's way of visually displaying that certain rows have been hidden since they don't contain the information we're looking for.

Pivot tables are a terrific method to organize and analyze data in Microsoft Excel. The more you know about them, the more you will get away with them. Filtering pivot table, for example, is a wonderful method to concentrate on certain data, and you'll frequently find this functionality included in dashboards. But fortunately, a filtering pivot table is simple.

Before we can begin filtering, we will need a pivot table, so we'll create a pivot table that is shown in Figure A using the data from the same sheet. In order to do this, go to any point inside the data set and do the following steps:

Select *PivotTable* from the Tables group on the Insert tab.

Click *Existing Worksheet* options in the resulting dialog to simultaneously display the data and PivotTable. Then, enter the F1 (in Figure B) just as the location.

When you click *Ok,* Excel will show you a PivotTable frame as well as a field list.

Build pivot table in Figure A using Figure C as a reference.

Figure A

	A	B	C	D	E	F	G
1	Date	Amount	Personnel	Region		Row Labels	Sum of Amount
2	4/1/2020	$1,208	James	Southeast		⊟ James	12256
3	4/3/2020	$1,434	Luke	Northwest		Apr	2643
4	4/3/2020	$1,587	Martha	Central		May	3882
5	4/10/2020	$1,435	James	Southwest		Jun	1347
6	4/28/2020	$1,523	Luke	Northeast		Jul	2434
7	5/10/2020	$1,596	Martha	Southeast		Aug	1950
8	5/10/2020	$1,549	James	Northwest		⊟ Luke	11700
9	5/10/2020	$1,170	James	Central		Apr	2957
10	5/17/2020	$1,882	Martha	Southwest		May	1942
11	5/19/2020	$1,163	James	Northeast		Jun	1476
12	5/23/2020	$1,942	Luke	Southeast		Jul	1925
13	6/1/2020	$1,870	Martha	Northwest		Aug	3400
14	6/2/2020	$1,347	James	Central		⊟ Martha	11767
15	6/17/2020	$1,476	Luke	Southwest		Apr	1587
16	6/30/2020	$1,767	Martha	Northeast		May	3478
17	7/3/2020	$1,370	James	Southeast		Jun	3637
18	7/11/2020	$1,925	Luke	Northwest		Jul	1460
19	7/19/2020	$1,460	Martha	Central		Aug	1605
20	7/28/2020	$1,064	James	Southwest		Grand Total	35723
21	8/4/2020	$1,680	Luke	Northeast			
22	8/4/2020	$1,605	Martha	Southeast			
23	8/19/2020	$1,950	James	Northwest			
24	8/28/2020	$1,720	Luke	Central			

Data | privot table | ⊕

Figure B

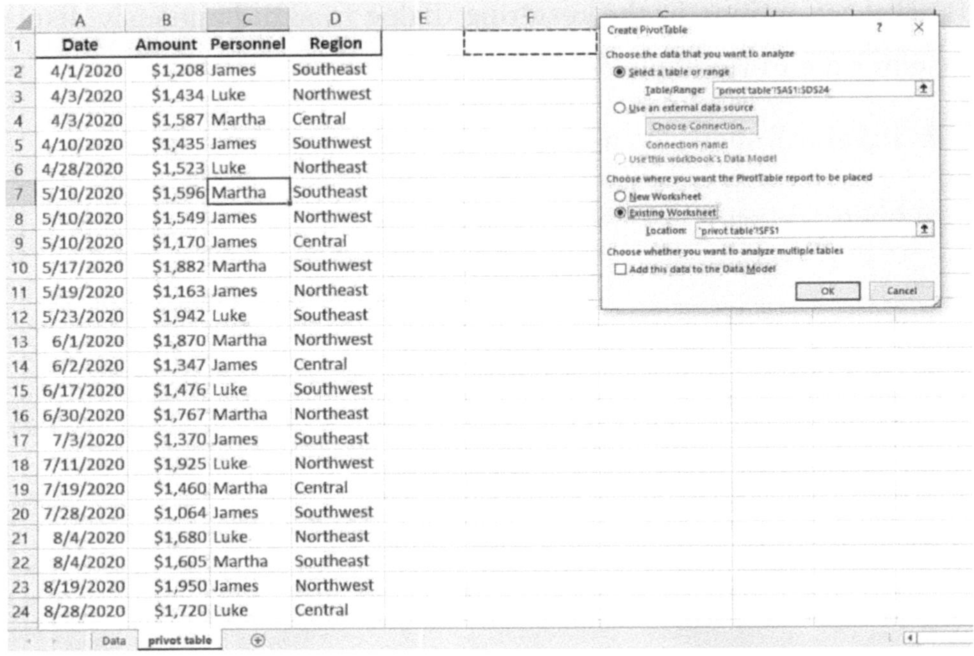

Figure C

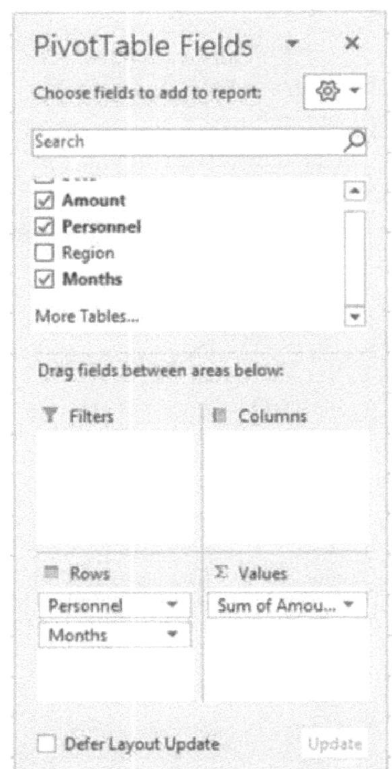

This more straightforward pivot table shows the daily amount for each individual, aggregating amounts that fall on the same day. Since there is a date, Excel automatically inserts date components, like a quarter, month, and year. The order of the data in data collection is unimportant. The PivotTable is an excellent report in itself. However, you may want to concentrate on specific data.

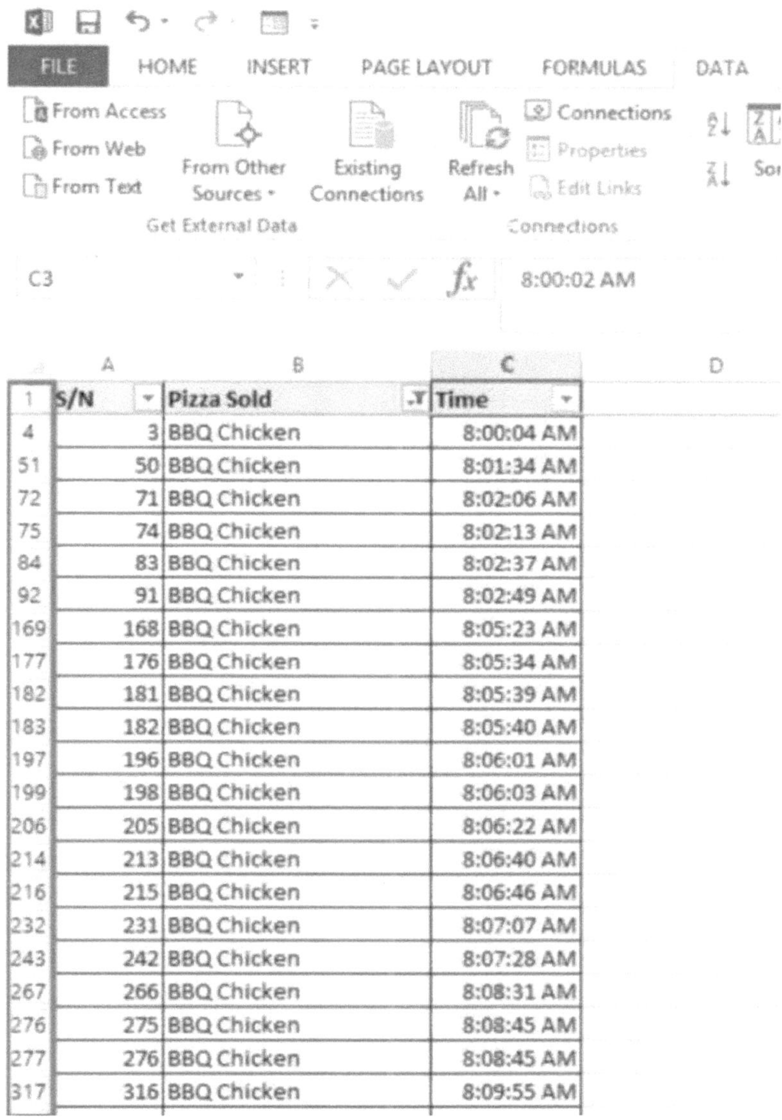

S/N	Pizza Sold	Time
3	BBQ Chicken	8:00:04 AM
50	BBQ Chicken	8:01:34 AM
71	BBQ Chicken	8:02:06 AM
74	BBQ Chicken	8:02:13 AM
83	BBQ Chicken	8:02:37 AM
91	BBQ Chicken	8:02:49 AM
168	BBQ Chicken	8:05:23 AM
176	BBQ Chicken	8:05:34 AM
181	BBQ Chicken	8:05:39 AM
182	BBQ Chicken	8:05:40 AM
196	BBQ Chicken	8:06:01 AM
198	BBQ Chicken	8:06:03 AM
205	BBQ Chicken	8:06:22 AM
213	BBQ Chicken	8:06:40 AM
215	BBQ Chicken	8:06:46 AM
231	BBQ Chicken	8:07:07 AM
242	BBQ Chicken	8:07:28 AM
266	BBQ Chicken	8:08:31 AM
275	BBQ Chicken	8:08:45 AM
276	BBQ Chicken	8:08:45 AM
316	BBQ Chicken	8:09:55 AM

Filtering is as simple as that.

1.68 Change Summary Calculation

By default, all data in Excel pivot tables are presented as the total of whatever is displayed in the table. Right-click on the data to alter the value and choose "Value field settings," which will open the box. It is a critical characteristic in accounting and financial analysis since it is often required to switch between units/volume (the count function) and overall cost or income (the sum function).

1.69 Two-dimensional Pivot Table

A pivot table with fields on both rows and columns is known as a two-dimensional pivot table.

Follow the steps outlined below to build two-dimensional pivot tables:

- Turn on the Datasheet.

- Select the INSERT tab.

- Select Pivot Chart & Table from the drop-down menu.

- Select all of the information.

- Choose the OK button

- With the pivot table tools, a new sheet will generate.

- Choose the fields you want to work with.

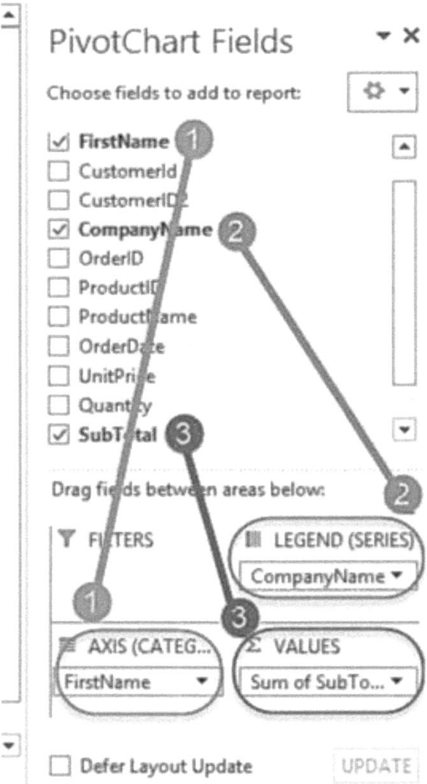

MACROS AND VBA

If there are multiple tasks to be carried out in MS Excel, and that too in repetition, then you will need the help of macros. Macros are considered a cluster of actions that you can execute as many times as you want.

The term VBA most likely refers to Excel's Visual Basic for Applications, a programming language to create Excel applications and Macros. VBA and Macro refer to the same thing. In this case, a macro is a shortcut for performing complicated tasks. For example, you can write a macro that copies rows from one spreadsheet to another and deletes unnecessary data. Macros can be created by going to the Macros command on the ribbon and following a few steps. You'll have access to VBA in Excel as well as other Office products so that you can create programs.

Codes that perform typical processes can also be found in Excel files. Such macros can conduct advanced categorizing and organizing chores and do a range of computations on the given information, but they will be deactivated by design due to safety concerns. Nevertheless, one should first activate macros in Excel if users wish to explore features, so you'll need to activate macros for a worksheet that utilizes them.

Developer Tab: The developer tab first needs to be enabled by a user as it is not visible by design in Microsoft Excel. This menu allows you to implement the advanced programming language in Excel, which is the VBA (Visual Basic for Applications) macros, the ActiveX, Form configurations, and also XML functions.

Recording and Creating Macros

To start with macros, you should first create one. Recording macros is considered the simplest way of creating macros.

Here is how it works:

Pressing the record button will prompt Excel to literally record all the future activity of button clicks you perform. Once you have completed the action, you can click on the replay button, which will cause Excel to repeat the set of clicks it recorded for you.

There isn't a more basic approach to learning how to develop macros in Excel than this. After you've recorded a macro, go over the recorded buttons to ensure you didn't forget anything. If you made a mistake, you can edit your recording, delete or add functions and combinations, and play it again to double-check. You will be able to understand the best way it works for you with practice. This is only one method for learning how to utilize macros.

However, there are a few functions that cannot be recorded. This is a significant disadvantage of macros. Recording macros is a good way to get started with the tool, but if you want to create a more complex function, recording your steps might not be the best option.

For now, you need to understand this simple and useful technique to record a macro.

Ensure that you have enabled the Developer tab in your application before starting. If it is not turned on, then you can go through the previous part of this chapter to learn the steps to initiate it.

Once you have enabled the Developer tab, move on to the following steps.

1. Open a new workbook in your Excel.

2. At the bottom corner on the left, you will find an icon near the word "Ready. " Press that button to start recording the macro. The icon will change to a small square, which means that the macros is currently recording.

3. Pressing that button will open up a Record Macro window. This window has various fields to input the name, location (to store the macro), and a shortcut key input for the macro you are recording. Either you can change the fields or leave them to default values. For this example, let us leave it as default. Press OK.

4. Press the A1 cell.

5. Type the text Salesperson and press Enter

6. After that, press A2 cell and type John. Press Enter.

7. Pressing enter will take you to A3 cell, where you can type the next name, let's say, Jeremy. Press Enter again. If you made some mistake, just fix it as you usually would do and continue with the next step.

8. Once you have recorded it, you can stop the recording by pressing the square button.

Now, it is time to view your created macro.

9. Press the Developer Tab.

10. Press the first button, which says "Visual Basic." This will prompt you with a new window. This window is known as the VBA editor in Excel. Depending on your settings, you may see different window layouts, but the options should remain the same.

In some cases, the macro may not be showing in the window, but it is right there. You just need to display it there. Before learning how to display it, let us first understand the various options on this window. The box on the upper left is known as the Project window. You will be able to notice all the worksheets of your workbook with the modules (macros are stored in modules) that have been created.

The window on the left at the bottom is called Properties. This window displays all the properties of the object that you select in the Project window. For instance, if you select Sheet1 from the Project box, then you will be able to see its properties in the Properties window. The box on the right, which is gray in color, is the window where your macro code will be displayed.

11. Expand the modules from the Project box.

12. This will highlight Module 1. Double click it using your mouse to show the macro on the code window.

You should be able to see the following Macro code as given below, if you followed the steps accurately.

Sub Macro1()

'

' Macro1 Macro

Range("A1").Select

ActiveCell.FormulaR1C1 = "Salesperson"

Range("A2").Select

ActiveCell.FormulaR1C1 = "John"

Range("A3").Select

ActiveCell.FormulaR1C1 = "Jeremy"

End Sub

You'll notice that Excel uses the Select method to select a cell based on the previous information you've been given. It records the value after the "=" sign for the property: FormulaR1C1. Whenever you need to input text in a particular cell, you will have to always add it within quotation marks.

The created macro will execute each code from the starting to the ending running each line that is missing a quote as the initial character.

Running a Macro

After recording a macro, you need to test it by running it from the Macro dialog box.

1. Click on any cell in the worksheet area or where you want to insert the text.

2. On the **View** tab of the Ribbon, click the **Macros** command button. Alternatively, on the **Developer** tab, in the **Code** group, click the **Macros** button.

Excel opens the **Macro** dialog box which has a list of all the macros you have created in the macro name list box.

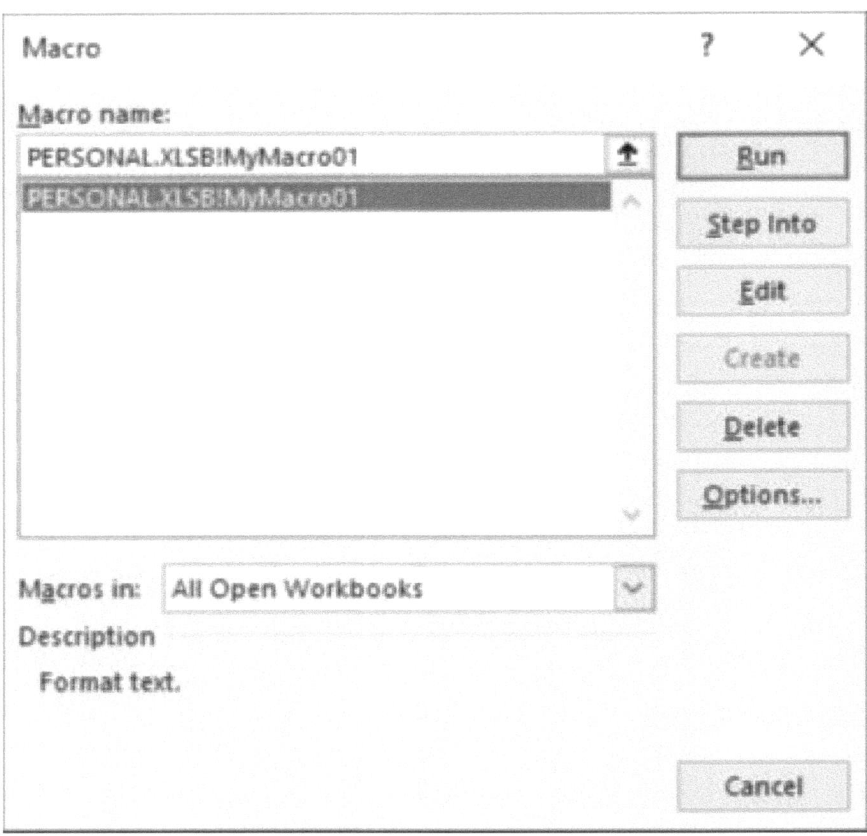

3. Ensure **All Open Workbooks** is selected in the **Macro in** dropdown list.

4. Select the macro in the list box and click the **Run** button. For the macro we created in this example, the name is *PERSONAL.XLSB!MyMacro01*.

The macro will reproduce the text *"Microsoft Excel Macros"* in the active cell with the text size set to 14, bolded, and the column widened to fit the text.

Note that the *PERSONAL.XLSB* prefix indicates that the macro was saved in the Personal Macro Workbook.

Difference between VBA and Macros

Note that these two are not the same, even though they have a close connection. People use the two terms interchangeably in various instances.

As mentioned above, the Visual Basic Applications is a coding language comprising of commands specifically for MS Office applications like Access, Excel, Word, and PowerPoint. On the other hand, Macros is not a coding language, it is a just a sequence of instructions that have a very specific purpose, which is to automate various tasks in applications like Excel.

In fact, a macro is a cluster of instructions that you want Excel to perform for achieving a particular operation. With VBA, you are creating macros and not using it directly to create operations.

For example, if you have read recipe instructions, then you can consider them similar to that found in Excel macros. The aspect that you need to compare between recipe instructions and macros instructions is that they both are instructing to perform a certain set of tasks. Achieving a particular goal through such commands is the primary goal of macros.

Although the language used for instructing for recipes is in proper English, VBA has its own equivalent for macros creation. Thus, macros and VBA have a connection, but their technicality is not the same. However, you can use several terms within the two interchangeably.

ACTIVATING EXCEL WORKSHEETS

The VBA module in Excel can be used to activate worksheets.

Press key **Alt + F11** to open the VBA code editor window. While in the window, enter the following code:

Sub Activate_Sheet()

Worksheets("Project1").Activate

'Or

Sheets("Project1").Activate

End Sub

This code activates Excel sheets based on the name of the sheet. You can also activate the sheet by referring to the sheet number with this code:

Sub Activate_Sheet_BasedOnIndex()

Worksheets(2).Activate

'Or

Sheets(2).Activate

End Sub

Tips and Shortcut

1.70 Shortcuts for MS Excel

Before diving into Excel shortcuts, it's good to go through the basic terminology for the various Excel components.

Any of the several boxes in the Excel spreadsheet is referred to as a cell.

Excel's active cell is the one that is actually chosen. There can be only one active cell at any given time.

The active cell, or even a group of cells, is referred to as a selection. If the range contains more than one cell, the active cell will be displayed in white, while the remainder of the selection will be grey.

A column is a collection of vertical cells in Excel that are referred to by letters ranging from A to Z. Excel can repeat letters a second time after column Z. As a result, column AA is the next column after column Z, preceded by column AB.

In Excel, a row is a collection of horizontal cells referred to by integers in ascending order from 1 to n. .

Inside Excel, there are many various types of data.

Text is a type of data that is made up of letters. Text data may also contain numbers. These numbers, on the other hand, must be used in combination with letters or manually set to text.

Numbers are data sets that are mostly made up of numbers. Number type data cannot use characters, unlike text type data, which does.

Numbers are used in combination with a currency marker in currency/accounting info.

Dates are pieces of information that represent a date and/or period. In Excel, dates may be formatted in a variety of ways.

Data of the percentage kind is a subset of numerical data that has been transformed into a percentage. These can be translated back into data of the number type and vice versa. When you convert a percentage to a number, the result is a decimal. Eighty-nine percent, for example, would be converted to 0.89.

You will save time by using the Excel keyboard shortcuts mentioned below. You may either scroll down the collection or use the Index to find the section you're looking for easily.

Basic Excel Shortcuts

These shortcuts are for Windows computers.

WHEN YOU PRESS THIS SHORTCUT	THE RESULT YOU WILL GET
Ctrl+W	A workbook becomes closed.
Ctrl+O	Option to open a new workbook.
Ctrl+A	All spreadsheet cells are selected.
Ctrl+P	A page for printing Excel documents opens.
Ctrl+H	Find and Replace dialog box opens.
Ctrl+S	The workbook you are working on is saved.
Ctrl+C	The selected text is copied.
Ctrl+V	Copied content is pasted.
Ctrl+Z	Undo action.
Ctrl+Y	Redo action.
Ctrl+X	Cut selected content.
Ctrl+B	Bolds selected text.
Ctrl+9	Hide the selected rows.
Ctrl+0	Hide the selected columns.
Ctrl+1	It opens the format cells dialogue box.
Ctrl+K	It Opens a window to insert a link.

| Ctrl+I | Makes selected text be in italic. |

1.71 Keyboard Shortcut

Before you begin, keep in mind that whilst the list is lengthy, it is by no way comprehensive. However, we've compiled a list of the most helpful shortcuts and hope you'll find them useful.

- Press Ctrl + N : Opens a new workbook
- Press Ctrl + S : To save a workbook
- Press Ctrl + O : To access a saved workbook
- Press Ctrl + A : Highlights all of the contents of a workbook
- Press Ctrl + C : To copy highlighted cells.
- Press Ctrl + B : To make highlighted cells bold
- Press Ctrl + D: To copy the cell's contents above into the chosen cell.
- Press Ctrl + F : To find something in a workbook
- Press Ctrl + H : Locates and replaces a cell contents
- Press Ctrl + G : To jump to a certain location with a single button
- Press Ctrl + I   : To italicize cell contents
- Press Ctrl + L : Opens the build table dialogue box
- Press Ctrl + K : Inserts a hyperlink in a cell
- Press Ctrl + P : Print a workbook
- Press Ctrl + U : Underline highlighted cells
- Press Ctrl + R : To copy the contents of a cell on the left into the chosen cell.
- Press Ctrl + V : Paste everything that was copied
- Press Ctrl + Z : To reverse the previous operation

- Press Ctrl + W : Close your new workbook

- Press Ctrl + 1 : Formats the contents of a cell

- Press Ctrl + 8 : Display the outline symbols

- Press Ctrl + 5 : Place a strikethrough in cell

- Press Ctrl + 9 : Hide a row

- Press Ctrl + 0 : Hide a column

- Press Ctrl +Shift + : Entering the present time in a cell

- Press Ctrl +. : For the move from showing cell values to formulas

- Press Ctrl + ; : Insert the date in a cell

- Press Ctrl + ' : Copy formula from the cell above

- Press Ctrl +Shift + = : Insert rows and columns

- Press Ctrl+ - : Erase columns or rows

- Press Ctrl +Shift + : Differentiate between formulas & their values in cells

- Press Ctrl +Shift +! : Apply comma formatting

- Press Ctrl +Shift + @ : Apply time formatting

- Press Ctrl +Shift + $: Apply currency formatting,

- Press Ctrl +Shift + percent : Apply percentage formatting

- Press Ctrl +Shift + # : Apply date formatting

- Press Ctrl +Shift + & : Position borders around the selected cells

- Press Ctrl + - : Erase a selected row or column

- Press Ctrl +Shift + : Delete a border

- Press Ctrl + Spacebar : Pick an entire column

- Press Ctrl + Home : Return to cell A1

- Press Ctrl +Shift + Spacebar : Pick an entire workbook

- Press Ctrl +Shift + Tab : Return to the previous workbook

- Press Ctrl +Shift + O : Pick the cells containing statements

- Press Ctrl +Shift + F : Open fonts menu under format cells

- Press Ctrl +Drag : For repeat a worksheet or drag and transfer a cell

- Press Ctrl +Shift + Drag : Insert a copy

- Press Ctrl +Up arrow : To go to the top most cell in the current column

- Press Ctrl +Right arrow : To go to the last cell in the selected row

- Press Ctrl +Down arrow : To move to the last cell in the current column

- Press Ctrl +Left arrow : To return to the 1st cell in the selected row

- Press Alt +Page down : To move the screen to the right

- Press Ctrl +End : To go to the last cell in a workbook

- Press Alt Page Up : To move the screen to the left

- Press Ctrl + F1 : For expand or compress the Ribbon

- Press Ctrl +F2 : Open print preview pane

- Press Alt : Open the control keys

- Press Alt +F +T : To use the options

- Press tab key : To toggle to the next cell

- Press Alt +Down arrow : To activate cell filters

- Press F3 : If cells have been named, to paste a cell name

- Press F2 : To edit a cell

- Press Shift + F2 : Add or edit the cell comment

- Press Alt +H +B : Add a border

- Press Alt + H +H : Choose a fill color

- Press Ctrl + 9 : Hide selected rows

- Press Esc.Enter : Cancel entry

- Press Ctrl + 0 : Hide selected columns

- Press Shift +Left arrow : Extend the cell range to the left

- Press Shift +Right arrow : Extend the cell range to right

- Press Shift +Space : Select entire row

- Press Alt + H : To get to the Home tab in the Ribbon

- Press Alt + P : To open the Page Layout tab in the Ribbon

- Press Alt + N : To open the Insert tab in the Ribbon

- Press Alt + M : To open the Formulas tab in the Ribbon

- Press Alt + R : Open the Review tab in the Ribbon

- Press Alt + A : Open the Data tab in the Ribbon

- Press Alt + W : To open the View tab in the Ribbon

- Press Alt + Y : To open Help tab in the Ribbon

- Press Alt + A : To open the Data tab in the Ribbon

- Press Alt + Q : To quickly jump to the search

- Press Shift + F3: To open the Insert feature dialogue window

- Press Alt +Enter : To start a new line in the current cell

- Press F9: Calculate workbooks

- Press Ctrl +Alt + F9 : For force all workbooks to be calculated

- Press Shift + F9 : For calculate an active worksheet

- Press Ctrl + F3 : For open name manager

- Press Ctrl +Alt + + : For zoom in on a workbook

- Press Ctrl + Shift +F3 : To build names from values in columns and rows

- Press Ctrl +Alt + : Zoom out

- Press Alt +2 : Save a workbook

- Press Alt +1 : Enable Autosave

- Press Alt +F + Z : Share workbook

- Press Alt +F + E : Export workbook

- Press Alt or F11 : Switch key tips on or off

- Press Alt +F + C : Close & save your workbook

- Press Alt +Y + W : See what's fresh in Microsoft Excel

- Press Ctrl + F4 : Close Microsoft Excel

- Press F1 : Open Microsoft Excel support

1.72 Tips & Techniques

1. Quickly select columns, rows, or the whole spreadsheet.

Perhaps you're short on time. It's not a problem if you don't have a lot of time. You can select the entire spreadsheet with a single click. To highlight everything on your sheet at once, click the tab in the top-left corner.

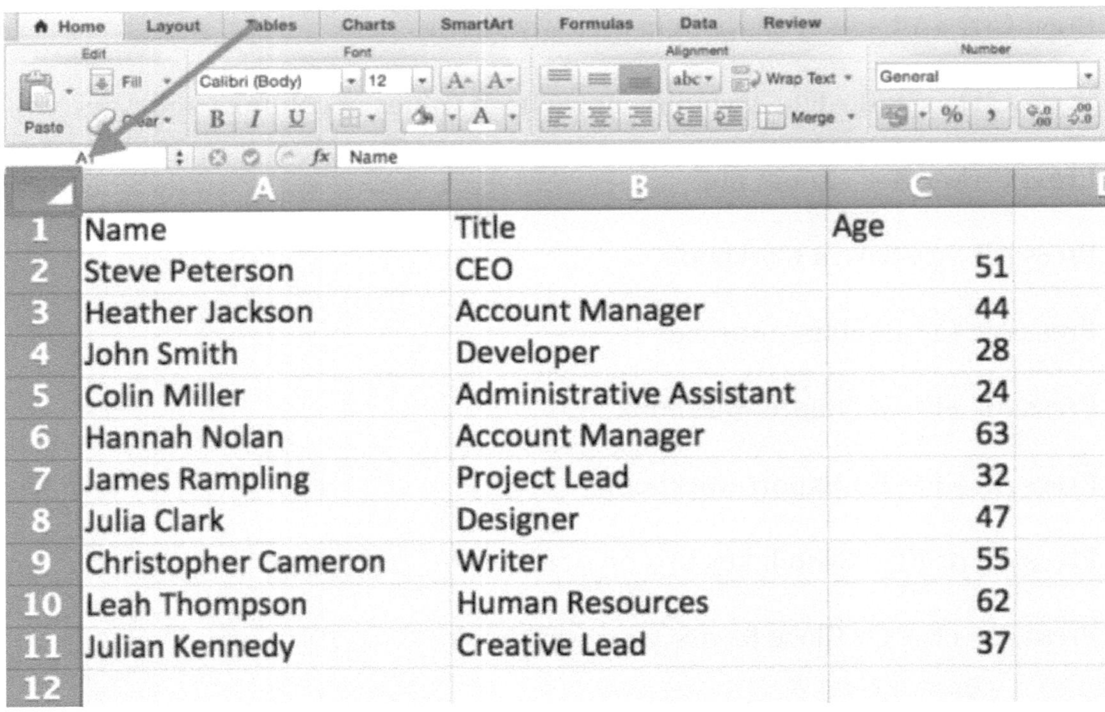

Do you just want to pick anything in a particular column or row? With these shortcuts, it's just as simple:

For Mac:

- To Select Column = Command+Shift+Down/Up

- To Select Row = Command+Shift+Right/Left

For the PC:

To Select Column = Control+Shift+Down/Up

- To Select Row = Control+Shift+Right/Left

This shortcut comes in handy when you're dealing with giant data sets but need to select a small portion.

2. Quickly open, create or close a workbook.

Need to quickly close, open, or create a workbook? All of the above acts can be completed in less than a minute using the keyboard shortcuts mentioned below.

For Mac:

- Close = Command + W

- Open = Command + O

- Create New = **Command+N**

For PC:

- Close = Control + F4

- Open = Control + O

- Create New = **Control+N**

3. Format numbers into currency.

Do you have unprocessed data that you'd like to add currency? If it's pay estimates, publicity expenses, or event ticket prices, the approach is straightforward. Simply click Control + Shift + $ and select the cells you want to reformat.

The figures would be converted to dollar signs automatically, with commas & decimal points.

Notice that this shortcut deals for percentages as well. Replace "$" with "percent" if you wish to mark a column of numerical as "percent" numbers.

4. Insert current time & date into a cell.

You may want to apply a time and date stamp to your worksheet while you're documenting social networking messages or keeping track of things you're ticking off your to-do list. Begin by selecting cell to which this function will be added.

Then do one of the following, based on what you choose to insert:

- Insert current time =Control + Shift + ; (semi-colon)

- Insert current date =Control + ;(semi-colon)

- Insert current time & date =Control + ;(semi-colon), SPACE, then Control + Shift+; (semi-colon).

Other tricks include:

1. Color Customization of your tabs.

When you have a lot of separate sheets in one workbook — which happens to many of us — color-code the tabs so that you can easily find where you need to go. For example, you can color code last month's marketing records red and this month's green.

To change the color of a page, simply right-click it and choose "Tab Color." A popup would appear, allowing you to choose a color from an established theme or customize one to suit your requirements.

2. Adding a comment in a cell.

When you want to make a note or apply a comment to a particular cell in a worksheet, right-click your desired cell and select Insert Comment from the list. To save your message, type it into the text box and then click outside your comment box.

A small red triangle appears in the corner of cells that hold comments. Click over the comment to see it.

3. Copy & duplicate formatting.

If you've ever spent hours editing a sheet to your preference, you'll admit that it's not the most pleasurable experience. It's really very tedious.

As a result, you're unlikely to choose to — or need to — replicate the procedure the next time. You can conveniently copy formatting from one section of a spreadsheet to another using Excel's Format Painter.

Pick what you wish to duplicate, then go to the dashboard and select the Format Painter choice (the paintbrush icon). The pointer can turn into a paintbrush, allowing you to pick the cell, document, or whole worksheet that you want to add the formatting.

4. Identify duplicate values.

Duplicate values, including duplicate content when it comes to SEO, may be problematic if left unchecked. Whatever the case, it's simple to find some current duplicate values in your worksheet by following a few simple measures. To do so, pick Highlight Cell Rules >Duplicate Values from the Conditional Formatting menu.

Build a formatting rule to determine which kind of repeated content you want to bring forward using the popup.

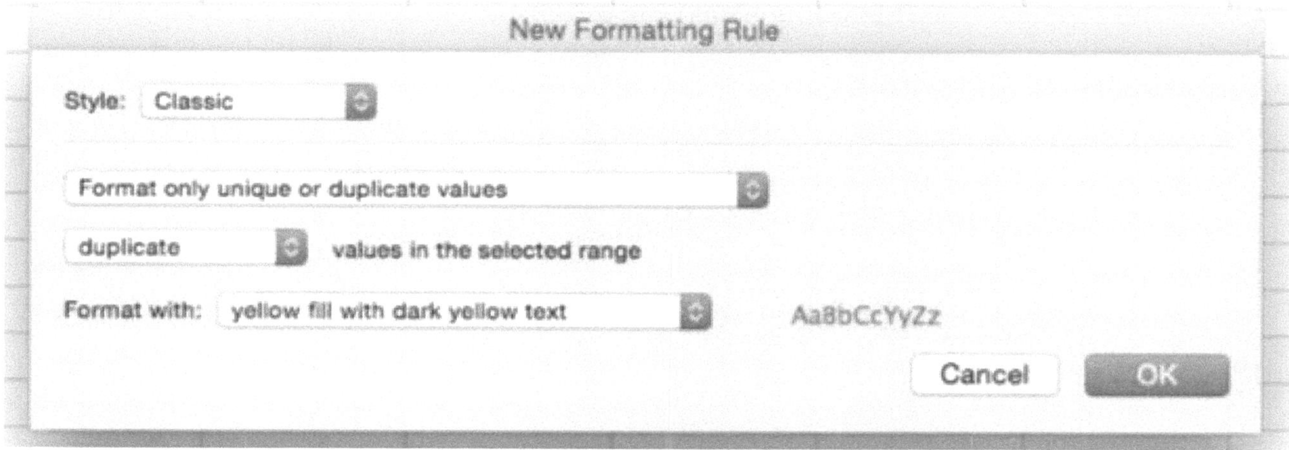

Formatted duplicate cells in yellow in the illustration above to distinguish any duplicate salaries within chosen range.

Excel is almost unavoidable in ads, yet with these tips, it doesn't get so intimidating. Work makes better, as they say. These formulas, shortcuts, & tricks will become the second standard the longer you encounter them.

1. Navigate with ALT in "The Ribbon."

The Ribbon in Excel 2021 applies to menu of tabs at top of your workbook (File, Home, etc.). Simply pressing ALT would highlight the relevant keys, which can then jump to specific ribbon tabs.

For example, pressing ALT and then M will direct you to the 'Formulas' tab.

By pressing ALT then using left or right arrow keys, you can quickly switch between tabs, while CTRL+F1 toggles between showing & hiding the Ribbon entirely.

2. Tell me about what to do

'Tell me about what you like to do' search box is a new feature of Excel 2021 that can be found in the Ribbon.

To get to it, click the box or press ALT + Q if you're using Excel without a mouse. The box is extremely useful for both new and experienced Excel users, whether adding rows or using VLOOKUP.

3. Excel New Tip: smart lookup

If you need details outside of Excel, the 'Smart Lookup' tool, which helps you conduct the Bing-powered online search without leaving the MS Excel window, is a new feature for 2021.

The 'Review' tab contains Smart Lookup, which can also be accessed through pressing ALT +R + S.

4. Automatically SUM() with ALT+ =

By clicking in the 1st empty cell in the list, you may quickly add an entire column or row. Then press ALT + '=' (equals) to add the numbers in each of the cells above.

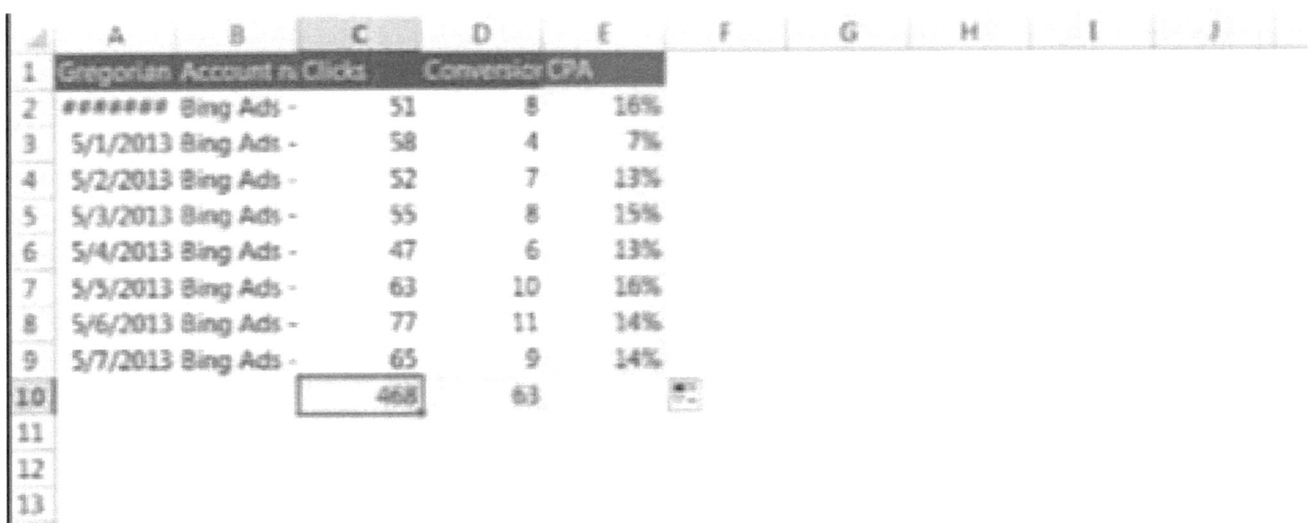

5. Keyboard shortcuts for Logical number formatting

Keyboard shortcuts in Excel can seem to be random at times, but there is a reason for that. Let's look at a case. The shortcut for formatting an amount as a currency is CRTL +SHIFT + 4.

While the SHIFT & 4 keys seem to be random, they are used on purpose since SHIFT +4 is the dollar sign($). As a result, to format as a currency, simply press CTRL + '$' (the dollar sign is SHIFT +4). The same goes about converting an amount to a percentage.

6. Display formulas with CTRL+ `

Examine the formulas first when troubleshooting errant numbers. By pressing just two buttons, you will see the formula that used in a cell: Ctrl + (also recognized as the acute accent icon) – this key is on the row with number keys, farthest to the left. It is tilde (-) as it is moved.

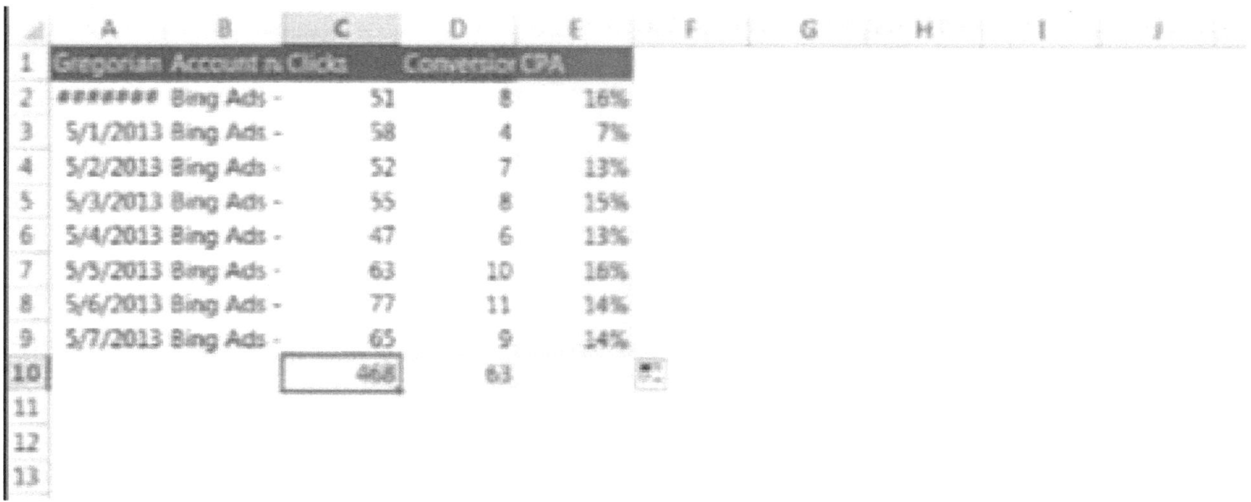

7. Jump to the end or start of a keyboard column shortcut

You've reached the 1st or last cell in your data set, which is thousands of rows deep. Scrolling is fine, so using the keyboard shortcut CTRL+ to jump to the top cell or CTRL + to slide to the last cell until an empty cell is the fastest method.

When you use this shortcut in conjunction with the SHIFT key, you'll be able to pick the continuous block of cells through your starting point.

8. To multiple cells repeat a formula

Never type the same formula in new cells more than once. This trick uses the same formula to fill all the cells in a column, but it changes to use the data particular to each row.

In the first cell, write the formula you'll need. Then, when the cursor transforms into a plus sign in the bottom right corner of that cell, double-click to copy the formula into rest of the cells within this column. The effects of the formula that use the data within this row will be shown in - cell in the column.

9. Delete or Add columns keyboard shortcut

It takes a whole day to manage the columns and rows of your spreadsheet. This keyboard shortcut will help you save time if you're adding or removing. CTRL+'-'(minus key) deletes the section on which your cursor is now located, while CTRL + SHIFT+ '=' (equal key) creates a new column. Consider CTRL+ '+' (plus sign), which was stated in a previous tip

10. Change the width of one or more columns.

It's easy to adjust the width of a column to match the width of its text to get rid of those #####
entries. Double-click the column's header as it transforms into a plus sign by moving the mouse to
the right-hand side of the header.

11. Recreate a pattern of dates or numbers.

Another fantastic aspect of Excel is detecting patterns in the data and transferring them to other
cells automatically.

Simply insert data in two rows to create the pattern, then highlight those rows & drag down to fill as
many cells as you like. This works for numbers, days, and months!

12. Use the tab key to navigate through worksheets.

With this handy shortcut, you won't have to take your hand off the keyboard to switch from one
worksheet to the next. Enter CTRL + PGDN to switch to the next worksheet on the right. By pressing
CTRL + PGUP, you can switch to the worksheet on the top.

13. Choose the format painter shortcut and double-click it.

Format Painter is a fantastic technique that allows you to duplicate a format in all the other cells
with only a few mouse clicks. Many Excel users (as well as users of Outlook, Word, and PowerPoint)
are familiar with this useful functionality, but did you realize that you can copy format into multiple
cells by double-clicking Format Painter? It's a great time saver.

Protecting a worksheet

If you have a lot of formulae in a worksheet, you may wish to keep them from being changed by
others. In most cases, your worksheet will include some input variables at the top. You may want to
allow those elements to be modified, but you may not want to allow changes to your formulae.

To secure a worksheet, do the following steps:

1. In your worksheet, select the input cells. These are the cells you want someone to be able
   to modify.

2. Hit **Ctrl+1** or go to the Home tab's Cells group and pick Format, Format Cells.

3. Clear the **Locked check box** on the Format Cells dialog box's Protection tab. Click the OK button.

4. Choose **Review > Protect Sheet**.

5. Change what can happen in the protected worksheet, if desired.

6. Click **OK** to activate the protection.

Conclusion

Excel is a very sophisticated spreadsheet tool for data analysis and reporting. After reading this book, you should have mastered the most important Excel formulas and functions, which will help you do your tasks more efficiently. Numeric, text, data-time, and advanced Excel formulae and functions were examined. Excel expertise helps to shape many careers.

The more you learn about Excel, the more you'll see how to use it in your daily life. Investing time in learning rather than squandering time on trivial pastimes is preferable. Recognize your obligations as a student and remember that education is more important than fun in life.

As a collection of data structured in columns and rows, a spreadsheet enhances the capacity to do computations more quickly and accurately. Figures, text, and formulae should all be mixed and interpreted stylishly and attractively so that the meaning behind the numbers is clear.

Throughout life, tasks and daily routines abound. The daily schedule of one person may vary from that of another. We must, nevertheless, adhere to it.

Given how technology has touched our daily lives, we can't picture a world without it. In our everyday lives, we use various technologies to make our lives simpler and more sophisticated.

Consider a world without the internet or Microsoft programs like Excel. The images would have a black-and-white tint to them. Consequently, we may infer that Microsoft Excel is essential in our daily lives. The more you care about excel, the faster you'll advance. MS Excel adheres to the same philosophy.

We also benefit from Microsoft Excel since it enables us to integrate Excel data into various apps, enabling us to increase our ability to access, understand, and show Excel data. To explain our PowerPoint presentations, we will utilize Excel spreadsheets. We may paste Excel data into Word or PowerPoint using the copy-paste procedures. Furthermore, we can password-protect our spreadsheet using Microsoft Excel, enabling anybody to see and print it but not make any changes. You may even save your worksheet as a template. Keeping our workbook as a reference eliminates the hassle of recreating a special-purpose worksheet whenever you need it. We can also keep papers in a variety of formats. If you enhance your excel abilities to the greatest degree, you will be able to work in analytics.

As we've seen, Excel can be used in several ways. However, we've only mentioned a few. There are plenty of additional motivations to achieve success in life. Excel improves our life. We may now finish a measurement without prior knowledge of arithmetic or statistics. Microsoft Excel is the only thing that makes any of this possible. Don't be the person who can't figure out how to use Microsoft Excel.

Excel is a critical tool in the business. It is utilized in the industry in various ways, depending on the firm. Excel is not often used in major

organizations. On the other hand, the small firm relies on Excel for day-to-day operations. The firm may utilize Microsoft Excel to create objectives, plan, and prepare, among other things.

The corporation can now successfully manage its day-to-day operations thanks to excel. Aside from that, individuals may be able to predict their outcomes. Excel's financial algorithms are operating brilliantly for the company.

In Microsoft Excel, the IF formula is quite handy for producing hundreds of justifications in business calculations. When it comes to operating a business, MS Excel comes in helpful.

All you have to do is go to the template menu to get the most out of it. Using a pre-made plan can eliminate the need to start from scratch. We all have monthly or weekly goals.

Consequently, we must manage our daily tasks to meet our goals using Microsoft Excel. In MS Excel, all we have to do is fill out the usual row and the comment column. We mark one of our regular activities as done in the comment columns once we finish it. It's also helpful in terms of planning. We will measure everything in advance using Excel as part of our preparation.

Printed by Libri Plureos GmbH in Hamburg,
Germany